THE BAVINO SERMONS

THE BAVINO SERMONS

LESEGO RAMPOLOKENG

ISBN: 978-1-928476-30-6
ebook ISBN: 978-1-928476-31-3

First published 1999 by Gecko Poetry
Republished 2019 by Deep South

Deep South
contact@deepsouth.co.za
www.deepsouth.co.za

Distributed in South Africa by
University of KwaZulu-Natal Press
www.ukznpress.co.za

Distributed worldwide by
African Books Collective
PO Box 721, Oxford, OX1 9EN, UK
www.africanbookscollective.com/publishers/deep-south

Cover design: Liz Gowans and Robert Berold
Text design and layout: Liz Gowans
Cover painting: Dolla Sapeta, *Mahoti*

to the thought control tower

please
let me out

i'm trapped
inside
your head

Contents

I

RIDING THE VICTIM TRAIN

Lines for Vincent

they pulled out his teeth
with a pair of pliers before he died
wrenched out his nails
'cos they wanted his manhood denied
they cut off his genitals
with a butcher-knife
while he bled they skinned him
& let the blood flow with the wind
i got the full blow of the message
in the red rage of a storm
whipping hard at the back of my shame
& still the shack of memory rattles its bones

let's put it in perspective
no one i know saw vincent's corpse
& the condolences were dry cleaned
by a military-man who lived
for the struggle to be human
yes the man in command made a demand
for his pounds of blood & flesh
we buried an empty coffin to symbolise
they say a jackal carried away his skull
was found choked on the bullet lodged in the brain
legend would have it
they waved his head in the air
& the bones would have made a throne
for the president
they mutilated & sodomised his dead body

vincent was my cousin killed by bravery
& a nation's homicidal glory

i showed him my first pubic hairs
& in the season of my confusion
he pointed out the path & how to walk it
but took a knock on the shock of mortality's discovery
on his feet with fog for a blanket
crept thru smog of a cannon's fartblast
to die in komatipoort
site of the seal on the settlement of deathexcrement
justice took a hit in the killing fields

vincent on a hill of scarlet
with the chill wrapped around him
it was a whirlstorm within
tucked under a blanket of fear
as murder's recognition grew
& still the wind of torment blew

at night i drown in sweat
with the sight of a death-grin
with a gun aimed at my brains
& they call that figment
of a fevered imagination
& still
i see the made up faces on the news
tremble as i watch them tuck into chicken at luncheon
in limosine whip thru function after
cameraflash function
& want to get their views
on why lives were compromised
but my questions are lobotomised

it's no use
stirring the grail of revolution

when all it can yield
is a landful of maggots in convulsions

the mother couldn't stop shaking her head
so they certified her mad
& locked her inside her solitude

the bomb bullet blade poison
or just silence
can ease the itching sore in my mind
as my tongue twitches
i know i might encounter the death
of speech
but it's said memory is a long road
made worse by the heavy load
of violence

Riding the victim train

I

blight on the site of the death-staple diet
at gunshot midnight
the leper cast out in the desert & cold
without snout or paw in the pot of gold
but warm & sane on the wisdom train
i'm beyond the boer factor in the kaffir sector
if it makes me suffer
rougher i come tougher
break its neck 'cos acting kaffir
is not being black

cry nazi riding tracks of the third reich
they stand back from the battle track
back up the second coming of the groot trek
herd themselves like cattle in the colour kraal
wearing the victim label
everyone a sufferer
pretending there was never a biafra
can't see ethiopia for myopia

kick up a rat racket
they pick up a rot packet
wearing skin like a wallet
riding a technic of pigment
moving from depth to platitude
selling attitude
each one a racial prostitute

the victims vie for martyrdom

blood is mud we trudge
call on history they reverse the charges
not jud suss but the birth of a nation
brutal equation

the mein kampf syndrome takes hold
my pain is deeper than yours
chained to history's flaws
from the root of the old
the fruit takes hold in the throat
then they wonder why some feed on the seed
of the dead

II

blight on the site of the death-staple diet
at gunshot midnight
the leper cast out in the desert & cold
without snout or paw in the pot of gold
but warm & sane on the wisdom train
i'm beyond the boer factor in the kaffir sector
if it makes me suffer
rougher i come tougher
break its neck 'cos acting kaffir
is not being black

but shame contained at dawn of conscience's end
old wounds dusted off   shown off
atrocity flags flown high
casualty squad on scar-parade
past afraid made present dread masquerade
achievement charade

relevant rule of the moment
tears dried out at birth
gorgon stoned blind eye devil faith
tears seen own corpses on the morgue slab
dr jekyll's back in the lab
dreams besieged in withering fright
vampires in blood hot night
unleash blistering storm on tattered flesh
rain of fire wash souls of ash
lives to the stake
a slice of civilisation power cake

bedrock of solomon
dread lock of samson
life's art strife's fart
beast to diseased heart
slow painstrain
death-flow-rain
hope in abortion
riding the victim train

A bavino love story at wet sunset

maybe she said i'm impure unclean there are moans & whores
make the most noise or give blows to the head of manhood
he said I come in molten lead striking a gong
when it can no longer claim to be long or strong or even a dong

maybe she guides him into her inner sanctum out of the storm
& he said when I pulled out to the surface I said shit & it was
holding tight when she compressed her sphincter passage
I could neither axe it nor run to the exit

maybe he said open the sluice-gates here comes the juice-flood
she said there's not a pole here anymore but a mole wriggling
around in the muddy hole & conquer was not an issue
the search was for the toilet tissue … (wipe away shame's traces
of aborted explosions when mossy walls of flesh layered purple
folded straightened out to fossilise shrinking shrivelling
in embraces of deep silences awaiting the final affirmation
in the after-mission)

maybe she said this is not right she tried a hold on the cold
in the heat & the night first she said let it be the last
but the genesis revealed her later splaying saying
stay a little longer but the morning crept up & stood
looking through the sweating window at their nakedness
& it was purity facing the dawn

maybe he said I page your flesh & read your need
see your reflection on my erection
hear your sheath call up my blade

& the sheets started to bleed

Wet pain ... tread with care

tattered rain
& i'm navy blue
in the frayed streets
pressure reaching down
& slow magic coming on
drum flute & the night whistle
mute music of torn throats

& then
tongues twisted around on themselves
spew out froth
green
rabid at yellow dusk ...

& the night gathers its red soaked apparel
staggers home

Ranterlude

still they sing

fronting
clowns chattering
break-down wet
sermon on the mounting & dismounting
to be mounted
licking the sting
out of each other's ding-a-ling
engorged each the other's wet nurse
gorged on a forged simunyeness

still they sing

dueting … dweeting …
semen drunken master & slave most trusted
faeces encrusted
together sunken in song
gang bang long
& boring
(until there's a hole beneath my sprong)
leaving me hanging swinging
from a brainstring

& still they sing

Love you in flight

1

burning behind my eyes & the smoke of memories
wafting through soap operatic skies
vile pleasures in / & the attic of dark pasts

bodiless fusses & the bustle of unruly ghosts
in the silent realm of the home & shelter dream
premature & dead nonsense in future virtues
excreta bequeathed ...

caved in emotion & the sword pierces flesh
sheathed between leprous lips
of this love song

2

amid everyday smells of dead gods
death makes more sense
in the fool's logic of life

3

heartsounds' incoherent explosion ...
orgasm
the fused light of the cosmos

& the whipsounds in church rang the bell
across enslavement's centuries
inhumanity's holy shame
& charred behind the smile of grace

paperhounds of the elevated domain
tell of death by eternal flame

scream & it bounces along
the halls of your mind
in turn sprawling
spreading
wide
whoring the existence principle away
& the reality bank opens its diseased vagina vaults
(molten balls & meatshaft chain between lips fallen apart
venereal)
to the money machine god's dong

behind steel walls of skin & tooth
somewhere our souls meltdown

Blue V's (for you my love)

views ... visions ... valentines
for the nightmare they said dig to the root of the deepest fear
it's there lurking
but i ... 2 ... i count up nothing poignant in anchors
rusting
3 ... 4 ... there's nothing profound in the sound of hearts
breaking
spirits in ascent whipped to death you're the phantom of my
dreams i'm the phantasm within your screams
in views ... visions ... valentines

vampires in my blood wolves at my feet on my skull sit
vultures but in my heart your call of the wild in my
mind ... i take them on one by ten multiplied by a coward &
smoke signals the way forward 'cos the love you speak
touches blue at the heart of my fire to life
in views ... visions ... valentines

but now life trembles on the back of bank-notes what stank
in the past is the present's perfume order is destruction
anarchy holy government the law an institution swaying on
pillars of abstraction an acute condition of putrefaction
of views ... visions ... valentines

perspectives shift & babies are caught in parents' teeth
ecstasy shivers down a scalpel's spine in the maternity ward
birth & death share pigment red is the core of our solar
system we dance to the rhythm of mayhem in a slashed ear-drum
view the sight in an eye without socket surround black dumps
with white flowers blood is a rain-shower the mind cowers ...
not cowardice but the dice rolling bones in the dust

eunuchs in the sterile street wave testicles in the
air in time for trophies
of views ... visions ... valentines?

from allegiance to rebellion is a fire-breath line
rein in mutinous emotion when wine in the glass is the
brains of my class ... swords tear through & crowds cheer
the butchered eyes of a child stare ... no more fear to spare
it's gone beyond a slogan where wounds stare back & wink
humour in a tumour
man's laugh is a gun's cough
take these chains off my brains I want to think of a time &
place that's sane
but it's not tears that carry pain my ducts are dug dry
the pulse of pus
the puke of my spilling ink
where I scratch pierce my heart to write & send to you my
love
these views ... visions ... valentines

& that's my end.

Crab attack / Intro to the master

baudelaire lost his hair in the rap-dragon's lair
ginsberg howled on the wagon running wild on jazz music
organic nothing plastic from the classics to the beatniks
oral poetics in the mix   colonial tactics fake the facts
i take it back ... a reappropriation act
'cos granny thought shakespeare a star player of soccer
but granny shocker lyrical clocker
dear oh dear she was a wild rhythm and rhyme rocker

i ride the mental colt break open info-vault
for self-rank pump system shock in kilovolt
jump bolt nut & lock on intellect bank
not verbal gymnast when I flip tongue it's toil
twist the WORD around dead in the ground snakes recoil
'cos i carry the sound of soil   now check it

grommit-food calls upon vomit mood
you omit the good become a sexcess-media-hype-fraud
dick your moses rod waving it in the face of god
commit your arse-pus to the masses
pass pads evil soaken
get the devil image broken
down to level baseness   madness
jesus me turn your back on the influence
cock crows in your face the consequence
scratch the surface & catch the dust
one with the essence i dance   beyond the crust

the new noah had no ark
i brought the dark flood
(now) you pen-draw my blood

culture-watch-dogs bark
drag my tongue in the mud
chains of thought rattle
you bring thunder to the mental battle
i ring lightning wondermental

pen & paper meet under blood-light
corner shit / writ-street & human mince meat
'cos lines i wrote you turn quote
get faeces praise paid on what I made
bum rush i mount you gush collect do a sperm-count
nightmare time   fright & scare —
no rhyme is a prophylactic
can't stop the pop-elastic gone ballistic
DO-RE-MI-MI-me solar you lunar-tic / lunatic
sick suck out my bone & now a clone is born
but forlorn duck stuck in the muck
'cos fuck is the spawn when creation-god's gone
lick it they freak it when I kick it (what ?)
self-SALE ON ROTTEN TICKET
stick it in out flick it roundabout till they like ape
bow cuntal scrape about shout MENTAL RAPE
it's grandmaster rampster first chapter mind captor lyrical razor
high art castrator
call me short-circuitor of the political vibrator
i come BEAM & BAM no
dum-dee-dee-dumb-nestum-child-amputated-thumb-to-hide-behind
no brain-bomb-rain i swarm
welcome to my mind
see tapeworm nerves squirm in the poem's come

i'd rhyme you from here to a nervous breakdown
but you premature-ejaculate on the first line   & go down

oops … wipe off & walk distant cousin
before I bust the next verse
call intelligence / riot police
lay a mental disturbance charge
& i'll still bring the barrage
of chronic cerebral discharge
little creeper on treble-rebel-route
hail to your drizzle i'm deeper than bass-root
nail in the tail in heat & sweat turd-flight
from pen-light
you defecate to my dictate
it's self-hate portrait
terminal parasite's self-spite
roast-crit try eradicate the host but later recite
'cos i'm scrawling the living word
you're jackalling   giving head   to the dead

I said baudelaire lost his hair in the rap-dragon's lair
ginsberg howled on the wagon running wild on jazz music
organic nothing plastic from the classics to the beatniks
oral poetics in the mix —   up & down & OUT

Habari Gani Africa Ranting

(eureka europe gathers the dust of a fallen berlin wall
  africa rolls in the mud of its tropical brain-fall)

habari gani africa
so free & unconscious where you sit
drowning in complacence's shit
a national situation its universal station top of the pops
pulled off the shelf when the rand drops
it takes a self-exultation / struggle ticket to ride the train
fortune-wheels in cranial rotation
slaves of example now masters of spectacle
hoarding seed crushed in loins labour broken
his / her / its imperial majestic(k) token
vacuum cleaning out a skull turning the brain cocaine
spliffing powdered bone / membrane rolled up in a dollar bill
terms of revolution's dictation not for negotiation

habari gani africa
government's hammering & anvilling consent
quoted out of pavlovian con-text
self aggrandisement's god complex in torment
self-eulogises til images of own creation believe the guise
soulthiefblindbelief demonsermonmindrelief gnu consciousness
in bloodstreams loo crass reflections of pork righteousness
nation's birth's midwife's face upon currency
wrath's head stamping the image-making of democracy
historical revamping drumbeating politicking
upon a slime bomb's ticking
bent-backing for international mother fucking
epiloguing your orifices puckering to nuclear waste puking

habari gani africa
operation eradication death movement's in stealth
declaration of good intention by tin-godly decree
mortality a military spending spree of corpse-wealth
morality's education for the living in health
a spiritual fulfilment read the gospel of saint general
in the satan staple book-write of denial
smiles of mirror practise / tv screen cosmetise flies on disease
spotlights out on melting americanised scream / ice-cream expression
& fatsweat's a sweet taste to thirst of emaciation
dark incontinent orwellian sequence content in emancipation
liesmacks soundtrack the powermonging in conference
crack-polished-bone-mirages affluence & wretchedness confluence

habari gani africa
for everything the media sells
foul winds of small change fanning both flag waving & burning
on both sides clogged-up brain-cells
commerce's judas coins always spinning
tails or heads of state turning
& vanity before humanity only beasts beauty contesting & winning
sankara-sermon-legacy's silent witness
wash our marks of millennial cains in blood of self-sacrifice
adam-father's sin-seed nakedness in the skin of his genes
fallen smashed upon eartheaven's kilns to fashion artifices /
edifices tegumental monuments luciferean at human genesis
graveyard upheavals of self-revelations

habari gani africa
dross rehearsal in cock-suction for intravenereal progression
a grain of wheat away from maggot-fat down six feet
land of sunshining on the aboveground in starleading roles
cold deep inside butt-plugged holes where scarred souls sit

scorncobwebbed for intestincineration by nuclear excretion
amputated arms held out for world rank alms of bob or two doles
fake deliverance in providence's corruption
bred on breadmoulded destitution
not diarrhoea or constipation your innards revolution
birth of the incubus bursting out of the umbilicus in eruption
commerce acidsluiced out your intestines
barrenstoned from lusty look of land-barons' medusa concubines

habari gani africa
criminal-against-humanity-element become celebrant
hour of the serpent's servant in power's fervent dance
to the slashed drum's heartbeat in despoticardiac arrest
king-poet-pus sings president sore's praises
faeces on tongue's feet pound to the sound of a wound's abscess
stagnation's ambition putrefaction's ad / ministration
arrived as implosion of oppression's child
have you survived explosion of liberation gone wild
nightfly hover above deceit heated under muckiness' cover
new worldly empty embraces of darkness' lover
black despair / regency shame borne coldfear's catarrh as trophy
ignorance's arrogance destruction's slave-agent of catastrophe

habari gani africa
bloodstains on morguesheet sweat of impotence
born to die lie dead in the street the lie of omnipotence
scarstripes on the soul sign of demention / delusion
look of drugged minds hidden behind illusion
& outside the grenade-reality-cracked window the botched moment
licemen of the west bearing gifts rearing rifts of torment
come to perform reconciliation   a land's abortion operation
nuclear wasted to the world's acceptance / assimilation
a disembowelment your creation cursed to a braindeathblow

manchildwomanimal NOWHERE left / right / middle / O …
sixfeetdownbelow
glow longknifenightsessionsplashed blood droplets in the sewers
flesh pieces from crossed Xs / axes of man-made-wood hewers

habari gani africa
purification rite-sight / site unset for handheldfirstworld viewers
no hard meat & bone news chewers
parental guidance adviced to toothless pensioners of civilisation
radioactivation messages of rage beyond broadcast of the age
riding gossamer telewaves the royal educated savage
thunder before morning conceived of night's ravage
squash for wine the fleas on which you dine   serpentine
brine-soaken oaken to the druid broken barkbacked
dried-up spinal fluid hangs a lifeline / capitalisticked sucked bloodmine
mortality / age on mortgage steal-deal tables fangstacked

(eureka europe gathers the dust of a fallen berlin wall
  africa rolls in the mud of its tropical brainfall)

Visions of salvation

there's harmony in heaven
the citadel of meekness.

hands & knees they are licking
the menstrual flow of paradise.

wounds of the pierced cross
& the slurps are syphilitic tongues at work.

the demigods breathe fire
& freeze the heart.

there's an abrogation of speech
& dumbness is lauded by promulgation.

radars are flags no thinkers but tankers
not initiative but THE order.

the masses are climbing to righteousness
on their innards.

II

BELO HORIZONTE ON MY MIND

Belo Horizonte on my mind

The Breed In
heavy SUNSET sister centuries' toilsweat born
the arrowed life / strife question lodged deeper than meaning
we lick the death / dirt-seed of slime the times' sons of sorcery
steeped in evil faced eagle idolatry
spawned of marsh-bags' human identity forgery
mistakening the sigh of the wound between steel-pierced thighs
for a song of love
filth in mental cripples' embrace of religious treachery
abhorrent smouldering in pits of hollowed out inhumanity
slouching along the path to perdition's obscenity
bellies bloated with emaciation's incongruity
with smirking starvation gazing depravity blazing cold
as snake eye opacity crawling backward into history
on torn tongues of deranged tenacity in the strain
against self-emancipation staring into hell-shock
of our time's skull-grins fed full on warped attitudes
wearing dung-hole expressions fang sharp spiritual suicide
pierces thru to the otherside of existence
we grovel at the altar of slaughter's backside
zealotry's jungle animal raised succubi grunting our freakery
in approval at devil-child incubi sucking out our being
munching on conscience we've eaten fat all aspects of revulsion
host to repulsion & what is disgust on the dum dum mission
wallowing in waste we hum the harrowing gory gory hallelujah hymn
of our acute / chronic degradation knowing explosion from within
inevitability beyond question but listen ...
tremors in the depths of a murmur of discontent
the dead restless' premonition of terrible evil
flesh-reel to blood-reel the deal is open on a man-sale
in devil-lock with daughters of the luciferean monstrosities

torn from wombs with evil deliberation
disease intent pumped to be born in death-ridden tombs
we need no justification for deeds of reclamation
yet STILL i ripple with love-muscle tension
at the doors of your passion

    1

i never saw sanctuary hill
where the slaves looked out on freedom all around
but beyond reach
& slept my way to ouro preto
woke up to find the sun burning my groin
creeping down the intestines of dead men
couldn't scratch the scab of a memory mortally wounded
however deep the itch & severe the heat
cold settled inside the mind
i found out meat & blood get eaten together
in the land of the cannibal vegetable
the rhythm of death is a master ...
rattle mental shackles it works out sexual said freud the tornado
i'm afflicted with a scatalogical addiction
but then any imagination's bird has to come down in the end
so how much is "free"?
twenty tons of gold in blackness & security in a bloodflow
down in the mine of a dark vision?

    2

THE REIGN is blackness of luminous glow
the path brightening in broken tentacles
clutching soft petal open to hope's rain yet concrete
— the seizure of our own knowledge riding the gloom

thru the brainwhitewashing of morning's seed
we claim no emptiness in romantic conceptions
while our cowardice in hospitality's disguise is us vanquished
the flames of myth in purgatory have us tamed demons exorcised
the incense is on the carcass of caprice's condemned:
the flies home in on butchery … an injury in my mind
where prey's birds (of mere-force-of-crying-voice-unruffled-let-
alone-shifted-feathers) deep in our chicken-hearts test the
extent of patience & watch our childhood in worship pose stooping
to murderous gods scooping their deaths into the mouth & drool
the morning dew turned death-dry … the mother's corpse renders
heavy the atmosphere with stench even familiarity can't turn
perfume … drums sound in the distance of our past
the fangs / bullets pound into the flesh of our present …
& FEED on the unclotted blood of the day's offspring
mortality is a tourist attraction the south reaps harvest of
on the weight of a butchered past & clutch at no frayed straws
of victories from wars waged in our absence
& without seer's knowledge or even thought
of our posterity's existence
but it's the present we tread
where the boot seeks to kick the head that refuses to lick
into the ground … & so ask:
what's beautiful about the favela horizon
of frustration's million mountains
resting on tattered hearts?
in fifteen minutes of silence-exploded brain
we cannot capture the bahia experience of the centuries
pestilential torment OR nestle on the cradle
of purity's breasts turned powdered
suckled on a material poverty stretching across slavery's history
forever burning boiling welling with bleeding feeling
of a torn apart humanity

3

SISTER black-fire ... lightning streaked with golden suns
dressed in the white of oxum's child born at the meeting point
of the orisa's blood & dark clayed flesh
steelboot-pounded brain flowing to far sunsets
buried deep in hypocrisy of a ball & chain culture
swinging its hooks into our future
& still the vulturous famine of our souls so long imprisoned in
& become merged with anguish ferociously canine feeds
on our entrails in the flesh & blood suture
of our progress / forward motion : we are carrion
in our lifetime yes we know passion let in zumbi's death
screaming across the skies tearing at our forgetfulness
can we speak love to jackals hurtling at our throats
we are tear-powered knowing how greater is loss of self
still the wounds keep throbbing deep in our slaughtered memories
blot out the eternal sunlight of our smiles
we BREAK THROUGH even as electricity's corded paws
wrap around our senses steeped in sicknesses' rot-green
buzzing thoughts of coprophilia
we feed on the liquid excrement the stinking abdominal waste
of our diseased-bowel-brained past & present masters
when they feed on the aborted souls of orphanhood
rendered putrefied
atrophied at birth
yellow in the depths as the monster of annihilation
north of homicidal-lust's shamelessness in infanticide
still it's not with contempt i greet the moon
try to rise transcendental to the summit of the human experience
in the fetid bruxa's underworld shrine of shrill undead voices
i raise my eyes to the glow on the apex of hope

behold the iron in the fire of humanity's fashioning red with
manlife-fluid in torrentous flow
nauseous sights flesh stewing on the hot-plate of power
in furious feed mode grown bestial at the cannibal feast
the belly bursts open under the slash of carrion-engrimed claws
& the hammers fall on skulls tills ring / tally up the sale
& ANOTHER metal conflagration tale is told as of old
yet the earth folds cold into itself

4

architect of my dreams
deep predatorial attitudes drag us from highest altitudes
of self-respect to levels of our own phasma beam out verminous
spectral we dabble in excremental experiment with our spirits
the whole edifice of pretension comes rumbling down
I break out in spasms plant dreams reap the reality of fantasy
harvest land truth exists beyond the mere factuality of lines
figures numbers symbols & mathematical calculation
what i feel is made real by its own definition
make no pretence to any great sense
wedged in the chasm between reason and thoughtless emotion
& fear on both sides of the fence
rabbits in the woods the wind carries our smell to the wolf-pack
the sweet smell of verdancy that cloak of foliage
sprouting colourful is deception
shall we say the blizzard of sound in the underground
is lizard harmless while the nocturnal rustle slinks towards us
at hunger-speed
the silence of no breeze is surface tranquillity
bound to burst listen & approach with caution
the breaking stems are necks twisted & cut
at its core faint stirrings of needles sharpened in stealth

with a smile the blood pours forth from wound
the bend in the road (to oblivion) is NOT the end
these days i walk the land in a trance
memory of you dances in my mind
merges with my every thought & melts into the walls of my skull
gives out a heat of intensity so severe it pushes perspiration
out from inside my cranium someone possesses my soul
seeks to hide my thought from me in the dark
i strive to only drop off when the sun reaches the peak
of its one-track minded chug across the skies
while the earth ever turns around
trying to scratch its back bite its tail
i go to bed with my head in the sling of a song
see the sun rise & fall & know i'm trapped between your teeth
feel like your breath holds my respiration
i'm breathing thru your mouth
soon the situation a point of desperation
puts a match to the thatch of my sanity
soaked in the gasoline of my illusions
then what volcanic eruption all consuming flames
for a taste of the recent past
but then that's not rationality
where i fly my flesh for a mast on your ship
& the slave-bending whip cracks & all whisper their penance
& none hears too engrossed in self-preservation
we are our own slaves screaming
from behind the walls of individualism
the doors are shut tighter than boa constrictor embrace
the main disc in our system's dislodged
my mind's blood engorged as the sun breaks in flood
turns to mud the dirt & crimson sweat of a neck breaking
in fruitless labour of fear
run down with motion of an enslaving ocean

& it's illumination:
the light in dark empty sockets of a corpse
trod real prodigious inside the maze
of ignorance-locked-head … lost

5

laugh like a cyclone in the face of hate's drizzle
is no over-kill leaves us instead crippled
'cos no holler or bawl can bring down the walls
life falls with the structures
we're spectres of derangement our Jericho lives inside us
forever chained to the yoke that is ourself
nothing all-hell christian in evocation of purgatory
just a vision of the lavatory hissing with scarred souls
eyes starred with lies of promise
the torment of the age knows no limitation
no incrimination
we rhyme our radiance / radiation with the fright of immolation
night IS light the end of inherent guilt
i wax incoherent in shivers of emotional disorder
spiritual battles waged where my brains burn
tremble in the grip of anonymous fevers
furnaces leap into life on your face
our birth is from the fiery pit yet we babble out self-disgust
the virus is deeply entrenched we self-destruct
on the embrace of a satan of a rotten mind's creation
& EAT the bible then flush ourselves down the toilet
with our shit of self-disfigurement
to live up to images of our enslavement
know rage impotence we are rendered sterile
in the thrust of scalpels of our ignorance
mutilation is born with our children

imaginations killed in the first moments of brutal existences
my son draws the future splashed in scenes of torture
blood is drawn i offer him gore for guidance
no protection yet for innocence
& yet NO celebration of desolation
cerebration deep within the daylight rays of night strike
where the roads are churned flesh-tarred
with those who slaved & brought us to this dead-end
where the light-bulb breaks inside my head
& the murderous night cuts at my taut heartstrings
stretched in memory of you i weep for aborted suns
in your eyes my loved one in your sight i'm purified

6

so the country knows only the sweetness in poetry
"LOVE runs deeper than VERSE" is ruby lipped proclamation
perverse the devils of pretence call up both those names
writhing & vibrating within heavy-charged silences
behind the brain in electric motion
but the dove drowns in its own faeces in war-time
across the planes through oceans & over mountains
hurtling to hell with no stories but bubbling under
deep in the flood yet heavy with emptinesses
uncertainties solid as frozen blood the age wells of emotion
i run my soul/lines to you in reverse
"eu estou frustrado … english english … all the fucking while"
so you turn walk away out of it
but the presence is forever there always near …
someday words will NOT be language
we'll occupy the spaces of our deserted hours
riding our dreams thru the great beyond
across the ocean of disillusion speech has bred

i'm a living shell's animation in my walk
rotten cadaver in motion in my talk is the sound of the dead
as the minutes tick away so the flesh of my life runs astray
where i shit / spit / slit out what i write to you
why we have to speak is testament of the negative patterns
of rule & control drummed into our being
society gone sick on itself
the foundation is what we should be on
exist beyond the deepest recesses of imagination
need no shafts or pipes of language to mine that
nor to search in our memory banks
for forgotten words to pin down what is more felt than said
often the word is void bouncing around head to head
where the need is to pounce on the mind
lost in the distance between / spinning off out of existence

7

"DON'T TOUCH … !" "look but don't taste"
indeed the age of exploration led to the carnage of our nation …
the ships the whips & the flesh that opened up to admit
the seed of its own emasculation
yet sanctity is personified beyond the stars
& outside realms of the universe
still your feet tread firm on terrestrial sticks & stones
across the barbs hidden under the roses
nothing romantic in fact kick sweetness in the teeth
in this time of bile we're fed
& vomit back into the mouths of death-gods
astral yet earthbound we invade to reclaim our own abode
stay little sibling my ear is tuned to the song
of your dignity straining against the odds
holding your eyes in clamps of lead

shall we go blind into the storm
knowing bowed-head's time is dead
forever bemoan the poisoned spring of origin
oppression is not a foreign concept but so deep within
we don't recognise when it manifests itself
on the plains the fires of deep malevolence burn my brains
illusions slither thru a hate-hardened heart
memory of the mother forever holds the child hostage
& prison often presents itself as a site of protection
& yet respect is paramount in our order of things
your place is sacred outside this terrain of hatred
the skin of age we should wear on the outside
not in the heart of the soul …

8

does aloneness mean solace when man & nation need not hold us
yet solitude is mere mental attitude as of seed thrown & so sown
the prison-planet that is earth's domination of twisted births
& the sorry death need in a world bred on mortality is …
the streets are over-run by hysteria the virus of control
is in the rule of the barrier between man & man in the terror
condemned's area zone in where we burst apart
under the slashing knife of a deified MISERIA
between thought & action lies now the moment gone
yet still we say prayers to the worn out history books of a
devil-mystery's spawn
as the blade falls on the head so life spills its guts
& we eat our own intestines on quests for the spirit's salvation
life chokes itself often the street kills its children
& they rule the dog-land which in turn eats & excretes them
out in gore-street
jump on the back of the human mind

slip torn hands deep into the empty pockets of our hearts
& we clutch our souls tighter than our nun's fear
of existence's rape ... don't shed a tear
or turn inward from what could have been
daughter of the light sister of the dawn
my bones turn to paste in the heat of the emotion
what horse carries its own cross across the mind / head / land-scape
of psychological rape
your beauty resides deeper than the skin-cover
on the horizon lies my own mental pollution
it tells of the putrescence at all levels of human relations
the landscape is without life-shape
still ... are we slaves to society's rules of conduct
subject to self-mutilation in our own denial
held in the penal colony of a plantation mentality
which states & legislates the amount of emotion to give
& the way to do it & the place for its practice
human happiness should always rule supreme
not resident within the codes of subjugation
entrenched by civilization's modes of non-communication
i hunt for life beyond the confines of words
drummed into our heads by putrid systems of human government ...

9

the tear ducts dried out with the hidden terror of the land
we hide from the sight of PUTREFACTION
at the rotten foundations of the nation
take ourselves on the ride to the ultimate high & low
find that bus of pretence stuck
the rain is pricked pain but as yet it lays down
the monster in hibernation ...
someday will banks burst larva bubble forth volcanic

from its lair / latence
spew its own guts to the sky as it flows with the fire
of shattered mysteries
the rock is hard behind the eyes i know
the body folds in vain self-fortification
but wait a little while
then … the trumpet sounds of self-knowledge
we meet ourselves at counter-point
the earth no longer turns around
but faces itself square & full in the face
the blow of recognition tears us out false senses
of euphoria & its vile twin complacency
the aura of blood digs up our blocked-up noses
flying in bits & pieces in the broken fleshed air
permeates / penetrates thru the leaden fortress
of treacherous silences …
then will tears be unleashed

10

i carry the dark concrete mist of my race inside my head
& it suffocates
the miasma within rises from the grave i cart along
malodourous i'm walking decay vast ancient barbaric
in colonial books they define the continent
in the philosophy of arrogance
& drumsounds blood pounds mad rhythms in my senses
heathen indeed
so gunsmoke is scent hangs on the moment's olfactory
withers the flowers of import's held up white-peace
the jungles are dead but not in minds
still the need to survive rehabilitation of the victim
the penitentiary mortuary clean white walls in psychiatric wards

splashed with colour pasted like slime crawling thick dirtcoats
of human like i am spiritual burning at the stake
in the wake of hate's arrested reaction symptoms
my veins are a swamp contain the land's sickness
brains churn out unmelodic electrocution spasmodic chants
mentally i mate with poisonous amphibians
brain amplexus they croak the tune i hum in cerebral time
'cos i chanced upon my father's nakedness
saw a gas-bloated body writhe to the music of rot
salt filled my mouth with earth & i choke
this is indeed zombie time & salinity kills as always
the beat's changed the dance moves stay the same
tuberculosis' face i cough in time
to the rough vibration of … confusion rains / reigns
long after the flames have gone down
the burn remains constant serpent unrepentant
at the tail-end the worm rises above mankind
& man looks in bewilderment as it sinks hooks out of sight
& into your brain & sucks out senses says:
"what a gain in intellect!"
OR "sour … yeah yeah … goes with power!"
OR "sweet! … shit … must have been a dimwit!"
tragic the logic of death
the same magic casts you in flame
raises up bodies in arbitrary sequence to heaven
inside carnivorous mouths
the circumference is well-defined

11

trace the pattern of tears beyond the fear-clouds
in this harmed & dangerous season of raped minds
view the horror running out of eternal night's terror

& know the armageddon count
where we're falling down fifteen floors of suicide
guinea-pigs for powermongers / control freaks
the world will parade fanatical/polluted minds as genius
remember pavlov's precedents & the condition of the human psyche
yes we spin in the death-cycles
some even try to better murder in the name of medical practice
can we assess the situation when we're born into it
without intonations of sickness
running a single track of madness
thru our lifeless existence
we are allusion in distant lands alkaline
but shall we bemoan the mud of our creation
turn reptilian with blades turn our skin inside out
with chalk & whitewash paint over the image
the fanon vision slashed thru the veil
of the mad assimilation trick …
pushed over the precipice into the flaming gorge of insanity
love is dead in that setting of inequality

12

murderous masses of sound crash down inside my head
in the residence of my mutilated dreams
beloved your being pierces the eyes of demons
an exorcism explosion in the heavens
yet all around maggot-infested decadence hurtles
thru the public address systems the walking dead chant
the praises of mortality rotting down the walls of existence
"silence is the graveyard" it's said … what's the purpose?
shackland mentality amid the obscenity of opulence
desecration of the dead nation
whose necrotic youth hangs on the back of the bus to progress

& inside the old in affluence clutch their lives' purses close
sickness creeps thru the gaping pores of fright
settles in the system of eternal night
where heads shuffle shift & crawl before spite
on their ignorance slashed stomachs forever bowed to the ground
but the viperous & serpentine occupy the high rise buildings
reptilian thoughts are grenades on my senses ...
i've outlived pretences to glory ...
the story has fallen by the wayside
it was the birth that had us taken for a ride
i try to clutch at my land's innards to wrest a grain of truth
hunt for some faith in the race called human
BUT ... try to face the reality beyond the bigotry
of a slave mentality & you know there's no fraternity
except in the cemetery
hope has become a rope around the neck
when the whip continues to crack from high power-towers
crashing the lightning out of our bent mind-backs
in the liberation age i break under the weight of my own thoughts
the gunbark is our existence's eternal rhythm-track
discordance makes us continue to dance ... gangrenous
a cancerous growth ... implantations of death at birth
that is the essence of fate ... until WHEN?
before we feel our blood-wells stir deep
& pierce thru the maconha cloud burst from the cachasa surface ...
awaken us from centuries sleep & ring the bells
to swing from high amazonian trees the jailers of our futures
sunbleached beyond the white of our skulls & deceptive flashing teeth
that's the story our history tells around the bone-fires
but that situation exists only under our protective head-gear-craniums
still ... we are unconscious on our feet
who will give us a kick-start?

13

BUT sister of the hurricane-storm
the warmth of humanity wraps itself tight around my soul
it's the heat in your eyes of pain
not buckling down under the force of brutality's rain
that thaws the ice in my brains
knowledge that sense exists in some young ones around us
is antidote for the poison flooding my veins
balm for these wounds inflicted by the tribe of the serpent
those residents of foul spaces sick claimants to vileness
evil behind the smiles on their faces of innocence's talk in
syrupy tones of shock therapy
the writhing torment of minds in unease
persecution as the ultimate treatment …
injections of strife into the human stream
competitions on humiliation of human life
turned out like animal skin rags
into the dirtstreets for complete effect …
mind strictures call mental envelopement economic development
indeed YES there is movement in the thought-stampede
but the practise is the human kettle on the boil
shedding no vapour but blood-steam
melting the scream of cattle heads deep in the sand …
NO … the battle dust of slavery will never settle
while we pretend suicide doesn't exist
& learn a language we can't think in
& choose to use it for self-expression / abuse / repression
the WORD is a lethal weapon … permanence is pure romance

III

RANTS

To Gil Scott-Heron

(the revolutionary's now a pseudo-psychopath on the compact-disked
warpath)

RUN NIGGER RUN was inspiration injection
of the LAST POETS' intonation insurrection
gil scott-heron was suckled on
a mouth to brain respiration   rot's subversion
liberation doctrine   brought art to the fight
for immunisation against the degeneration
of garvey's children & the spawn of fanon
on the run from the super-duper-shit-man
now life's an acquisition
the unborn have to make requisition
the terror campaign's gone electronic
in the bionic generation   a computerised nation
that won't falter at the altar of self-immolation
satan collaboration   spiritual contamination
like experimentation with extermination
gil scott-heron   the revolution is on television

tricks of the triple six cripple mystics
at the feet of the crucifix   no place for romantics
relics of the FUNKADELIC ground on the FAMILY STONEd
HENDRIX EXPERIENCE had GEORGE CLINTON for president
in the street's PARLIAMENT
no relation to the white louse saxophoney man
but the one on the JAMES BROWN SEX MACHINE
salaam alaikum   MALCOLM-Xed the CLAN
into a BOO-YAA TRIBE of SHABAZZ
made the ENEMY go PUBLIC on bass
brought the PRODUCTION out of the BOOGIE DOWN

got the PARIS panther on the howl on the prowl on the tracks
of its JUNGLE BROTHERS become POOR RIGHTEOUS
TEACHERS not preachers of fractured futures
when WINTER IN AMERICA froze bloodstreams in south africa
gil scott-heron   the revolution got on television

we choke in angeldust   stars go bust
street art vision goes to rust
creeping up the aliment of the pop-charts
acting out industry designated parts
of self-emasculation   masturbation on the bbc sabc mtv screen
& flip flop goes the hip hop nation
in sudden homicide running down the blood-line
of the griot running riot from dusk to the AFRICAN DAWN
& they called it negroid hell descended devil child
but black was MALOPOETIC mental attitude
in FULANI frontal attack
in psychological genocide time
but now scott-heron, the industry's mutant children perform
a systematic life devaluation   coward-style
they defile then revile the warrior profile
& the revolution's pantomime is broadcast
in an audio-visual bomb-blast
gil scott-heron   the revolution is on television

switch off that shit

The Cry of Disillusion

boil-fortresses burst
wall to wall notions crumble
a miscarriage
where a larval flow of possibility
degenerates into dead-end putrescence

shot of crack to the brain
or crack shot to the brain
either way it spills into the drain
the stomach-heave-upward movement in vomit
is progressive
if down in shit
it's reactionary
either way it's motion away from complacency

dachau dresden nagasaki
the cry tears at my thought
the cry distraught blood congealed
the cry concentrated pressure camp dirt wrought
the cry crawling from the cross
the cry worming out of the grave
the cry crucified & splayed to all cardinal points
the cry at the centre of the earth
the cry cracks rubber stoppers at all heaven's orifices
like the senses of the universe

in retrospect … hopes of order
in warped revolutionary zeal … another shift in perspective

uproot the class
from the cosmetics
of its colour romance

luxury flights to fantasy land
this land's balanced on a bubble
one prick & we're fucked obsolete / extinct.

The Poem & I rant

from subaqueous habitation & psychoskies the poem & I come
to reclaim the kingdom of the storm
amorphous satanic devise lines vast malignant depths born
death-mist raised supernal grown
volant fluid yet black mountain hard
(my writing hand shakes your writhing mind)
from seepage whisper in caverns darker than human sacrifice /
coproreality imaginations
murmuring scattered mal / unformed pathetic in deepest unconscious
i've felt the poem stir from foetal slouch to sub-bestial ROAR
swell charge in EXPLOSION streetwards
(noises of the aquatic abyss
subterranean terror invasion on the reclamation route-mission)

ugly lines in my head   i rhyme-burst out of the charnel-house
slime pays ask gravediggers counting up death-figures
in the street I meet the dutiful dead
but snivel & it's situation terminal
& paranoid from the cradle schizoid ridden without a saddle
sin-child fallen from the butchered sun's loins
i stride beyond the graveyard & above all known spheres
when the galaxies spew forth the poison of the coming years

flaming serpentine in my hand the microphone slithers
i spit mental poison & the connection is made
shrouded in blackness superlative from air i materialise sonic-active

cerebral encoded i drop a dope hyperload power blackout mode
(press repeat & hear the blast go
into the distance of the present's echo)
from line to vein the poem flows

grab the lifesource & it's electrocution
the graph's gone insane the brain recites the crypt / creep tick
written beyond the bounds of the script
where the present is past has the living in the future
the legend is true the poem and i eternally stride
rolled in one in the midst of churned minds

Ranting to Base-Heads

1

bitching reaching high for an erection
sides switching (with an) eye on the election
now the aim is twitching trigger on your buns
born of violence power fed this drug
now you're gone high & off calling me a thug
but these lead pieces are head-up among your faeces
preaching how now you vision a mission of odd religion
fake peace prayer day for god grant your pay stay on the take
make pretence to stitching up the holes you open
in my generation

2

comrade one occasion under raid
now you race to invade for intrusion
xenophobe trace origin on the face of a slave trade doctrine
you sought to erase
grand monkey clutching nut-case
now (you) stand & defend borders / barriers
berlin conference masters pall-bearers made
the lesson is wasted now the dividend's tasted
that was guaranteed in the master's precedent
pride is excrement splashed across the pavement
the scale of progress in a presidential statement

3

peril on the stage
incitement to revolution an accusation
set on the level of the devil in a rage

4

media attack sees the poet's vision black
perception come to wreck
on the trip of a rocket with a rip in the pocket
the sight will slit out the socket
the one with the work gets no pay-packet
they rearrange derange industry freak him out
pay your money & torment show him off to your honey

5

emperor strip tease take off the garment
they'll call you bunny smut token
not hit or miss this death is a promise
never broken / not made to break
the bread of jesus they only have cake
crack a lack of belief this is a thief of life
gun-tote cut-throat graduate of the knife
man run under the gunreign of mary antoinette
now a silent screaming bullet in the gullet
you were dreaming of fillet in the wallet
creaming hullett's at the ballot
but now dread's ripping at the gut
red dripping out the heart
white rock bate is set on no debate
black jocks on my block take a bite
first she was saving it then braving it
he was craving it now both are slaving it
it's need at the speed of 60 dicks per hour of power
running into sycophancy's orifices
licking in high rise offices
suck-out for a fuck-bout with a pipe / needle's kick

6

tense ghetto boys & girls' senses in gutter swirl
will change's wind ever start its whirl
where blood-cough ashes to ashes close off the wishing well
now liver-spit flesh hugs the cash-pit
it's blood track rabies
where mud crack babies
touch the moon with a spoon upon a candle flame
a stack on the deck of an economic game

7

rewind my mind to where wish & reality mix /
mish-mash /
merge meet & mate
so i can stop staring down at myself on a supper-plate
it's no track on my street
where i hear the neck break
from the movie into the home it's cracking my dome
the jacks at the back become domesticated
thru the night & my dreams
infra-red light beams
turn nightmare ghetto streetechno (realities) sophisticated

Lull-ranting for a stormy skull

(for jean binta breeze)
radics of culture culled from marriage of rhythm-ravings

1

once it was we groped for root of fears
with hope for hose watered arid-ears
tuned to years that fell & rose
in a forest of spears
now tears are water-coloured to commodity
lament is whinge pose broken cheesy dittie
old rage wise now in coward cringe pace
sipping on the whine & prising farts open in duckspaces
chewing & spewing pig-notes in muck-faces
high-arting eyes out of dark skies' children
professing the profound talking rain of pain
that the leaf wins the wind leans in to listen
to the song of the underground
but still the swollen waters bubble boil break rise
& settle ample with venom in mother's bosom

2

the sons we've borne have grown horns
blown big in mute phallic tones
come suck the poison of capital's nipple
silence fills the seventh temple
we will a malcalm ripple kill
violence's mental cripple people
of eye-patched dawns
search for flesh harvest & bonespill

hearts rattle around broken ankles
miles to bow mouths in the lap of crap
smiles sow tongue-chains around necks
(fallen from freedom-hill now stretched to heal)
to yap in the throttle of a life-long nap
brother pimp-prophet calls upon a knife-dream
to cut open a strife-scream
the storm resident inside sister's prostituted gap
abba father's wearing rife death's silent night cap

3

in fire-flight from god's spit
(the monkey's sanctuary is under its arm-pit)
no light lives in my sight
cold / waters of hate have blown it out
see … smoke rises out of my throat
the gout-eye of night is sharp with spite
pierces the skull where I live a blight
tonight the sky is the colour of fright
these times wear plight's coat
we put it on with a banknote-rustle laugh
the god-finger writes a white-line-storm along black paths
it's the dread-lam melle mel caught sight of
WORD-sword-straight cutting thru the brainstem
to stormy seas we call home
where crimson pirates roam
but still blood runs back
from desert flesh-flood attack to loam

Ranting Epilogue (in the survival of the shittest)

(for Ngoaps & respect to Bra Sipho)

the tomb yawned before your heart / head silence was spawned
& still searching for a hold on the ascendant
& the itching womb of the dog-tongue fawned
not white cloak's mendicant ambition to a rag
nor disease facing the empty medicine bag
nor the van riebeeck pestilent / repentant serpent descendent
herded / rendered the poet redundant
not subterfuge / intrigue in political rig
nor any ancestral call / crawl in / to the kraal
of the army beyond the live-gig
nor race-rabid-dogs of lucifer's curse
ever barking & biting at your back
but the home-sound-track to your verbal attack
seized & settled you at death-ease
made crucifiction salvation / purgation
put judas on heroic-stuntman-mission-station
your vision of the genesis was not your nemesis

wisdom's utterers say you're safe-warm in the uterus
but dawn-son-fed predators turned vulturous liars
vampires & reptilian brine froze uterine fires
& ate you in & out of the grave
body-snatch mode for a salve-patch of rottenness
the broken mask of the hate-slave
who cooked you with the lie / eye-look of love
it was a mortal path your senses trod
not in mordant fascination /
sick seed of death romanticisation
but kinship oiled smile turned cynic-side

to defile glorious heritage on the lyric-ride
the domestic bloodhound sniffed in yr hour of bleed
& fraternity on lipid-stomach-slid to fratricide
& mortality tied your life to a hole deathwide
quagmired / cain & abelled brotherhood in life-smother-mood
livewiredeath-cabled you to worm-food
kin is sin when tongues claim to bandage wounds
but push the pain's blade / missile deeper than wrath
omega is alpha the righteous feed on sulphur
brimstoned to death
before birth on the crossed path
made calvary society's toilet in the putrid aftermath
spiralling away heavenward with the son of man
they shit in the hole they open in your soul
spit on yr spirit washed out in their pig's trough
& rush to grow fat laugh over your heart's dirt
snuff the candles out as they're lit
put your heat on ice & gloat on its grave-cold
count you out on yr feet
muffle your poemshuffle's drumbeatsound
resurrection time around
drink your wit & throw you up drowned
in a stink on the shores of vomit
the corpse is a cold-cash bought & sold gold-fang-hold
for the snake / dismemberer of the old in the fold

i remember & behold prophecy refold mouldy / moulded as foretold
here in these many souths
where some wither shifted in foul weather
some slither & get lifted to ether
somewhere they christ-massed-around
here we lay man waste(d) into the ground
under the life-mound-found

we gather the rain / grain of broken truth
bought in the death-field-street
& fire cracks open the night
to a soul-sear / crack-wounded sight
elsewhere they breakfast in flesh-of-jesus bed
here we break lust for life in dread
rake in the must / bust of strife red
serve human-fat on a dirt-bed to the death-mad

(RANTING EPILOGUE CHORUS:)
when the ill-dealing heal-killing
the pain-railing & insane-wailing
when the rife-rambling the life-gambling
is lost (run down) & won
when the conscience of the conscious hits the ceiling
& the birth-willing is done only then   (& when)
                    will we be human
                         (?)

Rant notes from here to dela

(seed to weed   need to greed   portents to heed
       signs unread   lead to bleed
the sea is red   the sea is dead   the sea is a chill
dread   bloodspill   down   mad-god-head-hill)

constipation bloated bodies occupation
beyond prostitution open lips of constitution
& human rights bill
the power-hall's fear blocked entrances
(of) rule & control's vaginismus
(where) power plays the ball of impotence
down death-trench-razor-bladed-putrefied-pussy-passageways
& deep-stench-decapitated-dick-head-ways
all i lick is the WORD
wrenched out of soil to toil inside the money-python's coil
dead heads towels for beastly bowels of blood-oil
a line of semen & excrement runs from president to resident
& deep in the hole & venom in ferment the serpent is unrepentant
                         seed to weed

lashes of state's articles
smashed up testicles twisted up ovaries
double-fisted calvaries avarice's inheritance
kisses you give babies sugar-coated diseases
flags human rags wave multi-coloured faeces
economic cut-up in pieces
i perform a script-tease
your guns sing let the peace increase you rest in it
a sure fire hit chorus my lungs sting in the heat
see the fire-pain not cease the blood-rain ease
until it cleanses the shitstains

off the curtains on your brains
a grue pyre to the new empire you raise

                                   seed to weed

rodent's habitation in conversation
bats fly out when you shake your head
nod & rats fall off your beard
leaven bread of heaven's dead
the silence within sends violence outward
suicide squad's BUST reward
what's dead dumb is what's born with a holler
lice under the all-flighty collar
bodies roll are dice for the almighty dollar
poison in your shit in the ground spoil turn the earth jelly
sit on your feet take the land's last stand
smelly on the whirly of pus-criminal discharges
seminal charges cannibal surges animal urges pig-mental-purges

                                   seed to weed

Rant bent & broken

[at the waste of a poet's fall]

the earth-son on the rise is lice in poverty's eyes
insanitation fleas' inhabitation of a man-heart
curdled brainfluid & a stained crass / glass-mind
senses in the sand of a coward's last stand
the surrender flag stuck up a rass-behind
humming the unholy hymn of the marred-mad
the scarred-scared   the miscarrybagged
& blood streams not creation-high
but ever deadsouthward on the low caste wind-bend
still i'm married to a love-poem's daughter /
bleed of no slaughter
even in the foul-mould / wolf-fold / howl-crazed-cold

1

talk to glorious chapters of the past walk gone lame
the hand-clap beat is diseased back-pat rhythm
applause has the poet deceased in the fame-flim-flam / e
hypocrisy's loyalty lets shame lay claim to acclaim
praise is c1angourous razor renting the air
airstrung to embrace serpentine commerce's smiling race
tongue-kissing damnation hung on the millennium's anthem
to a gross miracle salvation
from a cross that's political aberration

2

if no tearflood can wash blood out of the sun
can it cleanse the heart rinse the hurt

get the dirt out of eyes lodged deeper than sight
that have seen / sin in maggot manifestation
the leprosy that lives within human dung's nutrition
dead conscience has the soil grown fertile
salivation has us routed to a swell
we live & give drink & stink of the polluted well
hissing with the pus of multi-national laughters' spell

3

when our flow is foiled to senseless stumble
let no drool water seed shrunken on sacresy's fumble
divine brain-death mumble where birth-rainwater used to bubble
a steaming brainstorm upon fleshed-earth clawed to rubble
smashed the word-track's back they crawled top of the worm form
so if my lip starts to trip-slip
my mouth gone from artleap to fartlimp
my tongue slides from glide to a mindstill
my breath run to butt-smell & hell's rotten-shrimp-stink-cunthole
let no hot-mind-feed-sweetened venom fall
upon my wintered-soul

4

will the sacred waters cool the rot
boiling in the heart of the heat
of this dread-explode-divination
the salt-vision to our lot
                    ?

A Nesses / Lesses Love Rant

(for Shani)

my love lives where holiness is national symbols
fluttering in broken winds
waving from the land's seven serrated anuses
in rabies' pulpitbull WORD stampedes
running out of time out of tune off beat gangrenous
in heat & the zealotry dance
scarlet mooned to discordance
across planes of violence
lanes of crimson silences   cadaverous
in consecration's murderous places   conscience dies

my love lives where salt in wounds pushes out diseases
to spiritual injuries that stare from skinless faces
eyes crucifixed on pearly gates
to where the unformed foetus legislates
& armaggedon is final battles of the races
suns of darkness shine on sons of righteousness
upon flesh dunes awash in paleness
silhouetted on bloodsoaked horizons
progress is trudge thru slush of greyness
baby bones powdered under plunder's hammer of justice
& champagne brain rain fallen from heights of prejudice
nailed to a holy inquisition / occupation cross
prayer's face turns from the skies' kiss
& reaching for the soul is the god of eviscerations

my love lives (no lies spill from the mouth of a wound ...)
where paradise a corner of babylon i turn around
on the search for shalom on the lamb from the new jerusalem

scam of immaculate sperm tranquillity a bomb in the genitals
sanctity of electricity in intestines
refuge in incendiary arteries
lead-fire winged angels of biblical fiction's choice
in reality rain of corpuscles
gather up the mannaed flesh pieces
the jesused-blood-deluge dammed in a chalice
feast toast & drown in the flood of peace / scarlet oasis
chase horse-shadows of the apocalypse
gas leaks thru the massadaed carapace
hades both sides of the religious / human-headed-fence

my love lives   i hope survives   the hatred that is sacred

Ranting time of the dark

bridegroom of the infanticided dream
the rot of screams' harnessed visions
I catch voices thrown across oceans of the ages
in the midst of hissed out razor embrace messages
from sharpslicked tongues that kissed butts of satans
(cut the pretext's throat & the lines scream from the zenith
word-pictures flash random sequence hell-fires on earth)

throw the switch on all who preach
impeach all thoughts of anything to teach
stitch up the wounds doing the obscene sound-rounds
for the wail factor register all howls on the richter scale
                        (lord give us strength
                there's a dangerous text on the wavelength)
on the radio rhythm-nonsense slaves cluttering the airwaves
my delinquency's got me scattering the frequency
television's purulence has me outdoors on a bubble-brain hunt

brains strewn across the apex of history's empires
deep in the gut of the future reside past spires
born into shame & pretence driven to the something else
dwells in the lie above the life-aborting sky
to blaspheme upon the name of the eternal darkness' flame
flipped judas coins come up the silver-headed jesus
on the cross otherside the tails of golden serpents
dance eyes bowed before the rapmaster's presence
the wordsword is killing the moon
not vengeance-driven but lethal silence
in deathstruck terror eyes
that have seen the error of noise without substance
the played & the made in death-bout bless the dead god-head

with the human flesh sacrament of mutilation's benediction
the spite of the snake's spit on the flower
who dares the design astral pre-ordained in crimson
bares the mark anal-stamped on the fore-head in flame
six hungry feet of dirt to manskinpages in fiery disintegration

Chorus for the damned ranting

sick morning after pain of a dream's dawning

(wounds of wars unfought showing the shamming
bugle sounds of the bought blowing the scamming
riding waves of self-sell talk the scheming)

screaming thru the dreaming deeper meaning
than the reaping of this moment's weaning
gods of filth slaying their praying
murdersounds of children playing
violence's silences gunning after innocence's running
laughter black burning blue lead in the back turning
true to death facing
dread aftermathing a red pre-birthing
flowing with ebbing life-current of the weeping
departing in swelling sounds of the burning
within being
ill world divorcing
telling of sickness bursting
out from amening the blaspheming

might farming gone mind-field ploughing retardation sowing
fertile lie sing brainsoiling feel human-waste-sting
petrifaction planting ill vision rain falling corroseed springing
towards mortal harvesting greed's hauling hope's death tolling
station sizing upon economic scaling land heaving throbbing
pulsing erupting convulsing exploding question freefalling
by law jesus-sacrificed towards national myth's varicolouring
con-forming
jacket & tied up illusion building
sycophantic green tongues flapping

lapping young hope dung of dotard fantasy's crapping
sinking of the thinking senses boreholing
covenants amnesia skeletoned to deception's flagpoling
arseholing up to treachery's bowling
wine of morality / mortality's doling
flesh bread of slaveships' hold mentality's baking
steel of veins' cold plumbing
seven seals of slaughter breaking
the sword that's life's garden guarding
armageddon nights pinning
the mind down in dreams of sulphur-binding
-heavenly symphonies taking dead angel wing

Prayerant for the lying days

lord god of the spleen-rusted sword
for our belsen nights fallen on & off golan heights
puslights up the path to scalped visions' swollen sights
on seizure's road to the future's erasure
the death-machine churns thru fields of human
upon the split frames of nation offerings of sin
demons of the flesh & skin devil's own babies' mutilation
it rains in haemorrhoids flowing bleeding money-piles
floating hiv'ed on rubber dinghies of pricked condoms
licked kink-dom now lifestreams run their course
overdrawn at the blood-bank now humans are resources
cloned out of existence face the universe across plastic surfaces
entrails wirestrung to the heavens' sado-masochistic caress
haemo-electric power generation for opulence's cynics / sneaks
squeaks of commerce's floors gleaming with lymphatic wax
in the oedipus fix of the crucifix in a cervix
before nympho-vampires take a bitesip of testicles
we milk scrotals to scribble ineffectual scrolls
        last refuge of the reality vanquished
        the creation flame extinguished
        sanctuary from the all-powered-word-mauls
lord god most trusted of the blasted brained horde
now time skulled beyond might's high place of whiteness
mutations on all fours in holy blasphemy's death circus wars
prostration in profanity's headquarters
on abjection's hindquarters
cretins creeping up putridity's abdominal crevices
deformities in darkest recesses at the lord's service
WORD-fires boil brain to headwater
life gives decapitated head we come in grey-matter
bomb-blasts of plenitude emaciation fed platitude

scatter mindseed to imagination's wasteland
head-hooks for the state's bite human baited on hate
now i hear the brainstem break the nervestalk crack
& know all communication trains on track
on straight lines of the god-walk
superficiality's low level intensity talk of inequity
underside things bubble devil rage hit the raw vein-mark
vibrate sense of no identity in the dark

Rap Ranting

(for Siphiwe Ngwenya)

calling all saints & souls bawling hymns
& anthems of the slogan change
it's deranged power to the cripple
takes a ripple to make a storm
in stones on bones nothing atones
martyrs in the fire of the liar coward
saying forward! yet staying on the outside
of the rap-line
moving mouth first eating their feet
fart hot taking a run before the gun
it's the plight of spit
in the fairy tale mouth of hell
with lots of stories to scream shout yell
nothing intelligent to tell
     i'm rap-ranting

is the poem crown or thorn or crown of thorns
i was born without horns can't be a slave to the grave
in necrophilial perception
got to have reception for beauty
can't wait till i'm mister man the late
to celebrate the bird the bee the tree
in the imagery of poetry
but the menagerie of bigotry
racial harlotry in grey all round bullshit …
meanwhile the stench hits my nostrils with a smile
& i'm moved to rude boy murderous style
the same water runs from my eye when i cry
falls from the sky & i feel pain

when the rain strikes black in element attack
biological/germ warfare on the atmosphere
& savage the page
when i think in ink the mind shrinks away
when i say the positive i venerate
the negative can't emulate
          i'm rap-ranting

watch them creep to get the rap asleep
keep awake kicking tight poetic
on the steel flash scream track
don't snooze on the juice of defiance
or pose on the noose of a camera flash-light
'cos life flashing out won't make the news
produce the contradiction in a move beyond hesitation
underhand high position doctor-attends
a malice-in-wonderland's constitution
creation of a friend to fiend situation
expose the superstition
of the reptilian's repose
under the leaderman-god stoned nose
of senility's deification
          i'm rap-ranting

introduce the meat on the site of the knife tip
mass-produce / hook the worm
now we've got to jump slave ship
know the 7th wonder another god blunder
need not row across the river of corpses
in death-flow from rwanda
in flight thru the television
sight & foundsoundnoise of thunder
to birth-blow burst the banks of an unconscious nation

gone to putrefaction
calling out for toilet paper rustle rhythms
shit talk aesthetic become anaesthetic
the economic / tic will stick suck the organic
down to plastic / synthetic
                    i'm rap ranting

the soul was crash-randed to be sold
dollar billed & pounded to a kill-hold
until pain slashed thru to the vein of red-gold
& from the future into the past
the serpent crawls where the scrolls unfold
the stories of fake glories told
made up laid stock market floored out morgue-slab cold
in intricate slime schemes written white on tar
in rhyme-scars upon fallen stars
wacky wretched existence on a rack slides
to lackey-pretence & cooks the power goose
understand when yr desert-storm loose
as you dance-hall knock or lovers rock a hell-hock
let nothing sterile cover the tongue's cock
of the black star wet-nursing a baby lock
soot to the foot we're kin-
dread-spirit striking thru rock
to the root
on the steel-street-reality-line-walk
                    i'm rap ranting
                    out

IV

From AN ARTIST'S NOTEBOOK

A play, this land is the stage

one character's only duty is to run around the stage shouting amandla!
and other slogans throughout. that and the occasional stone throwing at
anything that moves. that serves as a breathtaking device. we don't want
him to die of sheer exhaustion before the main character — whom we'll
meet in due battle course — gets to him. and of course the mandatory
toyi-toyi. and then he'll also need an AK assault rifle.

this we'll have to march to the movement's nodding headquarters
to demand. for this part i'll need a well pap fed soweto youth. ah here's
our other main character. what? oh you will need a costume? of course!
comprising of only a headband. okay okay you don't need to crack my
head with that knobbed-kierie. a red one, significant of …

i see. okwe gazi el'qhuma li gwaz' inkanyezi … significant of blood.
i see.

its letting of course. then he'll need quite a few assegais, shields
and knobkierries, demanding therefore a physically fit hostel dweller who
knows how to bash something — preferably human — on the head until
long after it has stopped moving. he'll need a good voice to shout usuthu!
at every war dance and head-bashing turn.

side by side with him to add colour to the occasion, i need a blueclad
policeman who won't have a lot to do either. just ride around the
stage in an armoured van. shooting directly and incessantly at the youth
and his immediate surroundings. then i need a few fire tongued older
men to make hot speeches about traditional/cultural weapons. a few
skulls with brains — children's preferably, or very weak and elderly
people's — spilling out and police mongrels lapping these up will be of
some american-award-winning significance. a number of dustbins
overflowing with fresh corpses will be of great necessity.

the stage will have to be in ruins, burning, smoke everywhere.

the audience will have to make do as best they can. the audience
be warned, the likelihood of their joining the cast is very high. throughout
the play's run.

at this point i light a match and necklace a cigarette. the smell of burning human flesh is revolting. but i gulp it down none the less. it is part of the play. he wrinkles his nose at the smell. and lifts his glass to his lips. no! i scream and tear the blood-filled object out of his hand and smash it down on ... no, before that i look again and find no red inside, he looks at me, a jackboot-puzzled look on his face. after a while, "perhaps i better go home," he tells me. where is his home? i don't ask him but the thought jumps out of my stomach and has me running to the toilet before anyone gets embarrassed and moves with the time of my dysentery.

two men, white from the look of them, are on an electric light civilised swear campaign.

"sea kaffir! boat barbarian pora."

"sout piel! one foot in england the other in south africa bleeding penis in the sea!"

we look at them and they turn on us. the rest is best left unwritten. suffice it to say, that i thank them here and now for breaking the bones of our monotony. my knuckles are still painful from the flesh encounter. such sweet pain, such painful pleasure.

at the next bar lines are drawn.

"ya the zulus are dam barbaric. all they are capable of is murder and they take that for the height of sophistication!"

"we shall not be led by the nose by compulsively lying kleptomaniac xhosas! usuthu!"

"shut up you mountain monkey mosotho, the only thing you people know is eating cats and horses."

"oh ya, when did you ndebele cannibals stop eating human beings?"

"as for you tswanas and your snake skinny pseudo-intellectual sour porridge drunk above the rabble closer to the queen's pink arselicking bullshit ... "

"stupid like your worm eating ancestors bundu headed shangaan ... "

blacker than thou politics in a kaleidoscope country.

the ultra african comes out from under his grandfather's lice-infested loincloth and adjusts his tie, "shoo, it's getting hot in wonderland, switch on the air conditioner alice."

i am also part of the cast, needing to die on the opening night. or day even. or even anytime during the play's run. the time is not set. the dying is, though. this is because i need to dip my finger in my grave wounds to write the script. so i might even have to die before its writing is done. in this event the cast will have to make do on their own. that will not be difficult since the script is written daily across the face of this land.

Bongi

danger is an aphrodisiac, he tells me. thus they were at the height of their sexual dive when the bullets flew, when the bombs raged she gave birth in the bush, wrapped the child in an army shirt plucked from a dead guerilla, after washing it in the drinking water from her canteen. the second child she gave birth to in a refugee settlement makeshift hospital while her comrade kept guard.

in a corner a guerilla with a fractured leg clenched his teeth tight as his leg was amputated. on another pile of bedding a young child shivered in the grip of malaria fever. some comrades carried out a corpse with its head blown off. the baby was born healthy fighting fit. she carried both of them across mined ground and to the plane landing at the jan smuts airport of exiles and guerillas returning disarmed by leadership and government concord, where the cold blast of june met their homecoming. like the other june that was their exiling. but that was a hellfire burning a path through the jungles of stranger at town home hearts.

it pained him to say it. but he did.

he had never stopped loving the woman he adored before the eruption of winter dried faggots. lena. when he got home she met him with the same fire he'd known years ago. or so he thought. exile has a glamorous stigma. he went home with her. she paraded him before friends she never had when he went away. a few days put paid to it. he walked out and back to bongi and their two daughters. after boiling water took the skin off his face.

"what hotels did you sleep in in exile what countries did you go to …"

bongi menstruated in the week long heat of combat. when the ground erupted and swallowed whole bone and flesh the liquid ran out of her. she used tree leaves for pads. child of an ancient time. the menses stuck blood red to her fatigues. a face as red as the waste between her legs came into her view in her rifle's sights and she swabbed it. another one tried to dive and her bullet helped it on its way. still the waters ran in heavy flow. unheeded they stank the wind. with the leadfilled corpses. shrapnel grazed her thigh and red and red mingled as she fired. the ambush dropped dead. her unit pushed on. war is a reality that knows no embarrassment. no one said anything when after the week she painfully tore the leaves from her legs and washed herself clean in that limpopo of floating memories and corpses.

after the war, after exile, after armies and police forces and cold dark gunlit days and nights. his leaving blew bongi's sanity to shreds. she didn't know his coming. he went back home in the dark. evading chants of marauding usuthu. his red spotty hat tucked down to his eyes. he was about to knock when he heard a child screaming its life away. then the other child joined in and "shut up fucking shit wine" completed the troika and doorpiercing screams again made him hurl himself against the door. it burst open under his weight as bongi herself screamed. the children were on the floor. one clutching its throat. when it tried to shout his name blood bubbles bobbed out of its slit throat pipe and ran on to the dirty skinthin carpet. he felt stickiness grab his shoes when he ran in. gore everywhere. papa … papa … mama … the other girl was trying to push her intestines back into her slashed stomach. he had seen all sorts of death. this throttled his heart. his stomach constricted as his scream hit the distant wall. they were all pleading with him. it was in their eyes. the younger one held her hand out to him. before he could get to her a spurt of blood kicked out of her throat pipe and the hand fell into the puddle around her. bongi had missed her jugular vein. hurling "inkatha" in his face before she passed out.

they took her to a mental asylum. she's still there.

i reach for my newspaper and "twenty-eight people died in soweto last night as internecine violence spreads across the reef" another "coloured people came into being in south africa because european settlers raped our ancestors" the blood curdles "five more bodies were found in kagiso yesterday following fierce clashes between hostel dwellers and township residents" as he looks at me a ghostly cloud settles in his eyes. this is a dead time.

from Rainbow Revolution

a tap on my shoulder gets me turning and spinning, a mad earth. he's wearing red on his head! the assegais pierce my glass. it shatters spilling my thoughts on the floor. but the red is a hat, a sunbleached spotty hat, not a murder band. he smiles at my shocked glazed look and sits down. lines on his face, exile's sandtracks. the wasteland his face my sweaty eyes drag themselves across.

the coffins, two child-sized, they go down and the world is silent, quiet enough to amplify the sound of a teardrop falling with a giddy heated thud into the space between sanity and a time gone mad.

"i'll get you another drink," he says to my shaking body. my ears hear it but it's some time before it registers. only when he comes back do i hear it brimful. in the beer tumbling down the boulder in my throat. i'm scared. this time is horrors! depression.

this four-year-old boy, this one watching me trying to drink this warm beer, looking at me from the dusty pavement, he looks blank don't you say, like a judge's signature condemning me to eternal nightmares. he watched his mother pangaed to death, he saw his ten-year-old sister raped and her head bashed against the wall repeatedly until she died after being made to suck the cock of a black time. they made him cut his father's throat while they poked a spear into his side as incentive.

when the wind howled it was devil time. light, no, dark rain battered the roof. a woman's voice came out of the dark. asking for help. she was lost, had a baby on her back. when they opened their hospitality the dark night splashed itself red on the wall. relatives took the nervous wrecked boy in. they found him shivering and staring and screaming in the aftermath. every time a car roars past, every time a knock raps the door he screams all hot dampness unleashed and dashes his emaciated body against the wall runs under the bed runs out of the bed hurls himself against the window screaming all the torn and tattered flesh dressed in a natty while. innocence is evil, is mater to rape, to kill. love too. it's dread time.

a man and a woman lie charred. naked and still thrashing in each other's arms long after the bomb exploded at the height of their lovemaking. when it tore them apart it glued them together. carole king was saying she feels the earth move under her feet. they thought the earth had moved for them as well. it had. under their lives. on a booby trapped bed. when they tortured the old bedsprings they detonated the passion of hate. and the death that comes with it.

that boy, his eyes are blank, open, like his mouth, he sits spreadlegged, they tore his anus to thin fleshstrands with spears and knobkieries hanging heavy between the thighs and sodomy. the leader of the pack shouted "moffieism is not african" and fondled his lieutenant's penis under the table at the next day's press conference. news cameras thought the image best left uncaptured.

from Redeconstruction

she goes to the north and i go with her. we catch the transtate. it's a bus that knows only the colour of money. but only black skins know this. and she knows it too. the bus is waiting. i buy our tickets. "where's the mlungu going?" asks a fool. "we're going to the north." i tell his curiosity. "she's going to the north?" "yes, and i'm going to fuck you up" his eyes bulge wizened spinster size. "give me that bag" i tell her. she's ready to ask stupid questions so i snatch it from her. she pales. her bag is heavier than mine on account of women's clothing. and the money too. she's trying to prove something and i'm not impressed. all the women boarding the bus are heavily lugged. the men lightly travelling thank you. she seems to think it's a new fashion. i know otherwise. i've been watching the vultures descend. they are five and very keen eyes, and very nimble fingered. two passengers are chasing their tails hands on heads screaming "mali ya mina!" over and over again. now they gather around for a meal of pork. they saw her hand me the money, they saw where she returned her purse, they are ready to pounce. they take the cue from my tearing the bag from her. hei! hei! he's robbing the missis this thug is ... hei! hei! they converge on me and one jumps back surprised at the red trickling down his face. i know these ancient tricks. the blade sings silently and is joined in chorus by string of blood from another's shoulder. he screams, she joins him. bloody bitch! the others look set to lose interest. one jumps away with his jersey grown a tail, she screams, stupid cow. she started this with her "i hate those bleeding pale faces buses. we must travel as the people do" she's trying too hard to change her skin colour if you ask me. but you won't of course, since i'm writing and you're reading in your dumb little over-fed brat lounge. they scatter, i advance, they retreat, the hyena crowd with them. a hand touches my sleeves. reflexes the better of me i spin around, knife hand flashing down. i stop it in time. "lessee!" she screams seeing her own chiselling before her. but i've stopped the hand's advance. "we'll get you!" a dying horse's pride gives a final kick. the bus driver is smiling at me. "yeah, you did them right my brother, they are silly these things. don't want to work these prick pocket …" he prattles on, launching his tirade into outer space through a toothless hole in his face, i grunt and follow sue to the back seat. later she says. "i hate these privileged brats who go to varsity and join nusas and come out thinking they have all the answers." "well how do you expect a northern suburb child to get politicised …" "look, i didn't join nusas at university because i think it's made up of a bunch of bored rich brats out for a political jol …" i turn around and watch the greenery roll. our country is really beautiful. we are sitting in the bus and it's smelly. on the seat opposite a woman sits, fatter than the bus and breathing heavier than its asthmatic wheeze, blacker than her staring eyes. she stares that way throughout the six hours of our journey, taking turns with her about six years old daughter. like mother like … shit thumb in mucus clogged mouth. the fools in our midst spend less time on it, but that's only because they're men. i see them looking at us askance, making staring an occupation. sue finds it all an adventure i can tell, judging from how she outsqueaks everyone else. running her hand up and down my manhood when the attention gets concentrated. it's interesting to sue, it's a trudge through the jungle, the bus' rumble the beat of some lost conradian / african drums. the undergrowth pierces my mind's eyes, the roots run deep into my mindhole. i shudder. sue thinks it's the fight's reaction. i keep quiet. closing my ears against her school girl excitement. the bus smells of sweating earth, it drugs and drags me deep into sleep.

"i like the way you two communicate. i'm sitting here with you and can't see or hear you talking but you sue seem to know every time lessie wants something. you must have succeeded in probing the african mentality." our hostess is blond and says she's the college's resident radical. the students don't know a thing about theatre so she's taking them step by step up the stairs of the royal theatre. sue argues that theatre is not a building and funny costumes. she mentions the oral tradition. they intellectualise. "such understanding you've got you two, such a coming together of different cultures. are you thinking of fusing that in a beautiful euro-african cutey?" her words smile toothpaste, "molly, what-the-western-educated-liberal-bitching-shit-are-you-talking-about ..." sue is up in tits. "i mean the way you've been jumping up and down to serve his every unsaid wish ..." "look look, i'm the common denominator here, he came with me, i know you, he doesn't, so ..." "no, no think he's shy because he's an african and i've been staying with africans for a while and i know that in the company of whites ... look, i know how friendly, how accepting the africans are but ..." i laugh rolling around in the mud of my status. it's a squelch.

later sue is in bed and molly comes in, i'm watching roots. she wants a cigarette and "you know, i'm sick of being alone, it's a good thing you came over." her eyes and her haunches on which she's sitting legs wide open to the doors of heaven tell more. i close my eyes, proffering my pack. she's a long time extracting the cigarette, apparently she has to run her fingers up and then slowly, so slowly down my arm before she takes her cigarette. she moans deep in her throat. her fingers gain momentum, cover the same ground over and over again, then descend to my crotch. she purrs and it jars my senses. she leans over, closer, closer and yet closer until her breath runs warm down my shirt front. then ... a sound throws her up and on her feet and running away and my hand crashing down. a cat saunters in and licks my dirty thoughts clean. snide remarks abound when we board the taxi back. "so now the whites are using our taxis, hm, not only are they not satisfied with stealing our land ..." at the first petrol pump someone is hollered out of the toilet to come see this spectacle. along the way the couple next to us snigger. "ha! these ones are clever, grabbing black boys to safe guard their own interests ... well as long as our brother eats there's no problem but hei aids people!" in johannesburg when we alight a school-girl walks past with a friend and gives me an up and down look, "sies you no longer see us nowadays because now white cunts are on jumble sale pooh!" another puts in. "ha! i knew they'd end up coming down to our gutter-level. where did they think they'd end up?"

it's night. we're coming back from a jazz nightclub. saxophones and pianos ring in our heads. i play the drums, she mouths the lead guitar, we're jolly. walking through the yeoville park, five hundred metres from home, we see in the distance a cruising police van, we feel safe, and warm in each other.

from Into the Death Zone

the girl next door is gone crazed on soap operas watching celluloid
nymphomaniacs parading their sex of rottenness in purity of purpose,
doped hanging on to hope knowing her lot can only be poor. some boys
run in a daze after their days gone up in smoke of the truck they just set
ablaze in a portrayal of the rules of repossession. mother push me back in
but no … wait … there's nuclear waste in there. of the power race
machine. complexes tamper with my reflexes got to oil my muscles but
it's such a hassle to take on the fucked situation. on tv they speak of
hormones in a riot … someone's just kicked a man in the genitals & he
vomits thinking his testes will jump out of his mouth he shuts it tight.
they speak of virginal tightness where i screw my head in my hands until
it feels it'll run out of my cock. my commune's run out on the mission
gone after the fashion of all past radicals now they all queue at the gates
of the first national bank stadium hoping they'll be there when it rains
american dollars.

it takes shit to kick my art. & the smell of blocked sewer systems. my
rhythm was created in the toilets of the nation it stinks of the rot of my
society. immunising themselves against death in feeding on human flesh.

the land burnt the smoke rose to heaven & god licked his lips in relish.
the boys grabbed the white preacher put him under his car set it alight &
called him father motor mechanic. & the rosary wailed jesus screamed on
his bosom but the heavens didn't come down to put the fire out. religion
is the opiate not the fire extinguisher. he burnt & turned to char & tuned
his psalms black in his hour of need & the youths sucked in his dying
smell & took it home to eat with their suppertime pap. for some it was an
aphrodisiac, they went on a rape-spree. a white journalist was abducted
outside the stadium while the leaders made impassioned speeches about
racial tolerance within, dragged off into the bush, choked with her camera
straps, & raped by a gang of twelve. that was the lucky number in the

bible. jacob looked down & called them his adopted children. & in the northern suburbs they went grey when the "kill the boers" chant erupted in the living room.

once again scott-heron the revolution is in quarantine. revolutionaries act out a part on the television screen. i'm going in to the death zone.

fed the legend of the big cock, "all the kaffirs want is to fuck white cunt will you let a kaffir near your sister … ?" they grabbed a man cut off his phallus sliced off his tongue so they could ascertain the theory that they are inter-changeable. & of the same size. when it was reported in the news segments of the nation played with their own genitals. the semen dribbled down the face of the leader on television. he opened his mouth to speak of the revolution & the spunk rolled down his tongue. switch off & the fight is over. & across the schlupping sound miles davis blew his horn spurting black acid seed "whoever said blacks wanted pink fuck anyway …" & was destroyed when a white woman refused him one.

in the era of destruction mercenaries share the loot in a collection of human bones. in a selection of flesh pieces falling in to the jurisdiction of satan, speaking fraternity yet seeking mortality. they sneak to the limits of insanity. they laid a trap for my rap wrote the slate / testament of this toilet state. & now watch them catch the stench of my crap when i hit the hell-gates of hate. & blood & brain spill, more tales of death to tell. where i'm going in to the death zone, singing my own praises through the storm of this time. screaming rhyme-missile powered ahead of time. turning this pen to a grenade the page is a battleground & the stage explodes … guerilla's at the microphone! WORDSOUND has power in rapid fire action OR slow & hard aimed to tear the heart of the gun-tower apart. i'm going in to the death zone.

arts & politics … false start, the question is vexed. but they sexed up the situation right up the pop-charts, taxed the nation chewing on the juicysluicy bits & parts counting man off the shit-list at the feast of human meat. turning woman gun-feed-breeding-machine. & now senility comes with insanity.

& the youth is caught in a blind moment of old truth that "arthritis is a disease like all man's enemies not conducive to progress" so the smell of milk gone sour behind the ears rises in illusions of power strapping the elders / leaders on the rocking chairs of history. from high towers of rhetoric, onto the gathered masses beneath, standing on a veritable platform of the people, "we need new blood in ranks of leadership" comes tumbling down, great boulders of orders. crack the brittle boned back of the revolution's stalwarts. the need is the removal of all warts, even if by dint of perversion they actually beautify instead of off-setting the rot within. & by historical record commonly known if you digress from the road to drawn battle lines, you tread on a landmine. so cowardice runs helter-skelter to shelter in the welter of the folds of the masses. & i scream my hysterical irrelevance cloaked in pseudo-intellectual garb "they can't relate to the mess in the verse i create." but to quote a line of poignance got to dig deep into the mine of profundity. "the greatest one can contribute to the collective effort is the individual input." the lion stands alone, show your own true colours, chameleon.

it's the rise of the dogs of war on progress. in the heat of reform digging deep into human flesh, the snake tribe chant a fake vibe. on the march they change colour & form. they hide & hibernate from the storm. they wait for the pressure to drop. then hop on top of a people's loins & fake the revolution's orgasm. it's the hour of the prophet to come out of mysticism's shelter of complacence, shower us with words of wisdom to put the fire of lies deception & treachery out.

MAKE YOUR PEACE with the wine of your brother's blood, hyena of the earth. heaven is spread before the lord, his own tomb. reproach the living god, in this time of the dead. & a heaven of wood & stone cast in eternal flame. garrisons in a land of grain, peace. go to war my devastated nation, at the same time as you refrain from it. in shame. i said it in silence, let it then be inscribed on my tongue. the WORD pleased the kings & princes of time & place, but it murdered the children. the harem at the palace of justice struck me to impotence. god, shall you answer to your name, or does the shame of it strike you dumb? after all, you're the god of grace in silence. & justice spoke peace.

in DEAD MAN'S LAND in a land of the dead addicted to blood, where the earth spins on its rotten axis of red, in a spiral of disease pestilence & the violence of silence. it's said the instinct of the insect leads it to the dirt that made the pig fat. likewise the loud fart of pretence gets applause for the disaster junkie bawling for peace through putrid orifices that tremble in high rise glass tower offices of power polished with the gloss of decadence. where the existence of the man on the ground is mapped out in poverty & impoverishment become a holy concept.

in my country of christianity where the few hold a monopoly over the plenty in a pocket of humanity become a profanity. blasphemy in the mouth of a system of predation dating creation back to man's own apparition. where corpses roll on & bloat the land's death factory floor. but the law of the land, of supply & demand, calls for more of the gore on the sleek hand & sick minds of doctor jekyll & mr hyde the slaughter house from the world. merchants of death ring the desecration-bell of commerce in underground cells of covert operation, to balance the deficit their statistical equation of perversion on a pathological fetish's mission. it's a situation of putrefaction. the disease of ignorance eats into the nation in the storm of assimilation, some succumb to the glitter at the bottom of the gutter of human relation, pick up the flesh of their own conscience grown skeletal in the fruits of a revolution aborted in the explosion of greed's cannibalism. it strikes my typewriter dead, & the vultures descend through the fire burning through my brains.

from Doggit

a beggar peeps in through the open window & asks us for money. & the person i'm with shouts "waitress, there's an alternative customer at the window" & i think that's inspired & jot it down for future use. flesh & blood matter. good word!

what?

yes.

how's that?

it's this way. your god is an empty word given substance by the flesh of your sacrifice. a hollow word ringing across the lifescape. it takes human death for a voidal stomach's filling. many an eternal virgin licked his seed on the cross & yet again sucked his manhood in the tomb of blind faith. seeking solace in ignorance. but the courts of man don't recognise that as a defence. they try to shock him in orgasm out of death & end up with semen splashed all over their faces trying to embrace the second coming. i look at them & they come at me. the ground lifts under me cracks my nose blood spurts in a compact disc of joan armatrading asking me over & over again what do i want!

what indeed do i want?

"i'm your slave ..."

a whip cracks & a man is on his knees bound whimpering & paying for it even. wilfully contributing to his own enslavement. "lick my arse!" the prostitute orders him.

"yes ... yes ... my mistress ..." in fever & spasms of heavenly joy in earthly pleasure he passionately slides his tongue between the cheeks of her buttocks & ejaculates when she shits in his mouth. her lips are parted throbbing moist & pink & i step on them with a boot, blood spurts but is lost in the lipstick screaming sexism! ideological correction advances on me. guns sticks knives hand grenades all murder weapons of a nation's birth. all power structures are sex based. manifestations of the male humanimal domination-traits. the great he-man.

bombs hydrogen capsules bullets even deodorant cans for the disguise of the stench of the species' fears traumas evil thoughts & inhuman ambitions are phallocentric. the hand of feminism a moment ago clenched in a fist to smack my balls opens up in a flower arrangement in preparation for a resounding applause for myself-castration complex. the sword sheaths itself in a cunt. the scabbard is vaginal. the human head & therefore thought in macrocosmic principle is a male domain. & i can't think anymore. the pen is another aspect wearing the form of the mancock. it falls impotent spermless. fuckface!

they come at me. supremacists children of the god-rod-wielding earthlings risen above human status & standing in the mono-visioned sanctified strata of human class-base ... i take a sentimental trip to a hard reality. i want to sleep & i go down, hit the ground hard with my face. the perception of the rule is wrong. or is it the legendary exception? forward! progress is not subtle. it leads down to below the surface of expectation. about change! in attitude. we call for a revolution of all stagnant concepts ... without concrete focus. the rock crashed against my skull & the bovver boot cracked behind my cranium, jagged edge of broken tooth lodges deep in my throat, searing pain. i'm burning. sulphuric acid bubbles up from the depth of my shitfilled stomach. multi-coloured layers of sound & sight explode ... rainbow visions splinter. they're ripping at my flesh. the shattered window panes of my scattered thoughts gather around my feet in the dust run to the head fly through my mouth in the stench of vomit. & i laugh. the hyena night grates against my fear, & the cowardice allied against it. i am laughing from the throat to the vibrating brain catching in the fractured nose the pieces of my rotten senses. peace love harmony in the distant sound of morning coming through & the music speaks to me soothing.

& i gather my glazed consciousness around my wet feet & start counting. from one to the racial doctrine. newly washed & deodorised nazis on the rise. europe spills its pus into the mouth of the rest. there is neither east nor west now we need new compasses. cardinal to the anti-tidal sunset. change gear into definition time. i try to re-orientate myself in the coloured scheme of things. "black is knowing it ... is a state of mind. nothing pigmentational but outlook. is a way of life ... you could be navy blue horizontal ... reptilian cold blooded apparition it is mind based ... faculties shaped to the seizure of power ... the fear rearings ... you could be gutter bound spiritual grappling with false philosophies ... it transcends bounds shackles breaks through shackled mentality ... slum living squalid louse eaten feeding on your own brains ... could be down the line on the wrong side of dissent ..." on a street corner quest for your own shit ... the smell scuttles flies ... a rat wobbles on drunken feet a mongrel starts feeding on my vomit ... the concrete side to my mental putrefaction. a man initiates his son to the ways of the flesh like all right thinking parents. never ever fuck black cunt ... he drummed over & over again into the child's eternally nodding head notions of the black hole's powers of consumption. he opened with a chain saw a hole in the black maid's stomach to reach to the womb & stuck his phallus into the bleeding hole ... son you've got to reach their wombs without fucking them ... that way you remain pure ... & the son followed the father's example. at the expense of countless black virgins. but of course his major concern was that he couldn't tell if they were. promiscuity being an inbred part of the mud races. blood & torn flesh the son didn't find a major turn on. put his dog into the picture. put jobs-vac in the newspapers. invitation to a hound-lick-fuck. doggit!

the van rattled senses down the dust track. choking down sobs of tubercularity, growling grinding down gears. & the dog was in the back. sophie sat with the man up front in the cab. turning around often looking the dog in the eye. big yellow fangs dripping green saliva. like the stains of decadence. where the sun dipped ripping yellow liquid through the sweating roof. hairy hands on the smelling wheel whipping bestial around the potholed veins of the dirt track. shameless winks & silent snickers of looks full of lust & expectancy in the blue-grey in the moisture of the licking tongue in the distant gloom of smoke palls & sorrowed corn-heads hanging on the shame by the wayside.

visions & fantasies & yawns of tight clenched thighs where he placed a rough slithering sweaty paw on her trembling jobseeking thigh. the gates of the farmhouse opened wide. cavernous enclosure beyond.
you'll get into the house of fame if you do what i want. money & money four hundred a week if you do what i want … lots of money for close to nothing. in fact naked. truth naked. then he had her on her knees with thighs apart from what was to happen. on her knees & a whip at the ready he had her. don't look. buttocks & head licks. the wet tongue probing deeper & deeper further than eternity. slobbering in flood. arc your back bitch relax there's muscle power in liquid heat. breathing heavy skies clouded in silent thunder. when a dog stretches its hind legs shoots its pink head phallus out it's longer than imagination deeper than reality. the blackness was there. on its knees. thrashing in shame. choking screaming shattered mind in pain of the back taut in reception of a dog's fuck. when black splits it's pink. when blood shoots out the welts remain in conscience. deep etched. barring consciousness. the dog drooled on her exposed buttocks heaved deeper than forever hind legged to human beginnings. & the master's grin drooped to hell. lucifer do it boy! nightmare states of mind hallucinated past reality. it heaved grunted & threw its bubble load turned around dug deep into her flesh its paws for leverage & flooded the floor with saliva semen shooting through her wombed self knowledge. it snarled human its phallus growling to endless depths reached beyond she felt like it stuck in her throat. exploded lights of knowledge. shattering myths of civilisation.

filled her walls. still it was clawing at her senses. pumped beyond proportion. & the dog howled coming shattering down unloading its rocks. felt like they were glued to her walls. she screamed pierced the far wall. fainted on the saliva semen salted floor. the dog thrashed for a grip. anchored itself deeper & deeper in her flesh. & the man laughed &

laughed. pulling his penis out masturbating onto her limp body. extricating itself the dog went bounding out in release. she woke up on the edge of town with four hundred rand in her hand. & dry between the legs. she sobbed in silence with groceries in her hands later standing by the gate of her rusty shack as her two children ran to her smiles on their faces. & their scrawny dog ran between them. i've no reason to believe i wasn't one of them. & i retch heaving globs of blood into the gutter. terror fire ignited. & in the suburb the dead-alive arise. fearful of the great black danger. the all consuming hole in the sky. scared they'll be sucked up to heaven.

a white man hacks a black baby to death cooks it in a big black pot & feeds it to his children. that will guard them against the black spirits of the continent. the pestilence savagery diseased mentality of the children of cannibals. car-lights burn right into the depth of my mind. they're trying to read my thoughts. i've got vomit in my hair its smell keeps them away. the mongrel cleans me up. a distance away some dogs start barking.

Coming Down Bricks

coming down bricks. mammy beat me! imploring. or making a court statement. i don't know. mammy beat me! he crescendoed. the window rubbed my ears raw. but it was cooking my mind. it rose to a scream. the bricks came down. mammy beat me! it concussed my head. big balls of icy fire. it ran down my spine in a chill. the rain or the gurgling drainpipe in there i couldn't tell. but it froze my buttocks. the bricks came down the bricks came out. on my head inside my skull. the membrane between frayed, stretched, a tearing sound snapped my head back in disbelief. it was dark. inside and outside. inside the room outside the room inside me outside in the engulfing dark. one hit the back of my sense. my head hit the face of the window, both broke and shit! they screamed and came tearing out. bleeding and bloodied i ran, into the bricks. slipped and fell on my bleeding nose. rose half way and ran a step backwards and fell flat on the ice of my backside. mammy beat me. it wasn't a plea. i was just telling, no, screaming, clawing the skin off my mud coated mind to get to the clean bone. i don't know if i was crying, but my face was liquid. my hand came back red. it disappeared in a flood of rainwater, the red. the hand remained. and mammy was beating me. the pain gave me an erection. sudden, unexpected. the bulge in my trousers opened a hole in the mud. mammy grinned, her teeth were red. but she wasn't bleeding, i opened my mouth to scream, she snotted inside it. i gasped gulping it down. mammy sat on my face. the smell hit the back of my toilet mind. she ground her groin, my snake tongue went in, she moaned. and splashed her waters into my nose. she fell on me, digging me into the mud. the boy laughed, eyes red. and trembled taking his juice oozing thing out. out of its spout spurted white that fell on mammy's head. mammy raised her face to the sky. my head went deep into her bucket hole. take your finger out of my vagina! mammy shouted. my head jumped up in surprise, ah! mammy screamed. yes! yes! push the whole of your hand in. i got in up to my shoulders. he groaned, mammy moaned. flooding me. i passed out. drowning. in the mud. of discharge.

they pumped on, puffed on, in time to my moans. the boy was a bull, the girl a rabbit. he snorted, she squeaked. i held on, fast, to that passion's whirlwind. turning and twisting. it threw me in, beat me out and into the swirling heat. i trudged through the dust. it whirled into my hair, it got into my skin, it clogged the mind. that dust. the heat kept coming down. i dragged myself through its marsh. the car came howling out of that hell. of my memory. i dragged myself along. out of that abortion. the blood beat against my skull, the walls strained. i hit my head hard and it stilled. then the waterfall roared and hit my eyes out. it soaked my face, the torrent and the dirt soaked my shirtfront. i choked. big boys don't cry small men do. i throttled my scream. the boy grunted, the girl sighed. the juice dripped when the spell broke. the beasts bared their fangs. drooling. they came over. i was prime. and primed.

it was high powered pressure. the heat intense. swirling dust. it rose into my nose. i opened my mouth to sneeze, it hung onto my tongue. i gagged and it fell on my lungs. weighted, they dragged me down. but i had to keep moving. the sun hammered the centre of my earth. i carried its weight along the road. load in me around me. eyes slits to hood the heat the dust out. it pierced in and through. a thicker bellow of it, the dust, whirlwinded in the distance, coming. around me the country lay sprawled, yellow in the face of the elements, defeated. a few shamefaced shrubs hung their heads. droop-eyed. a tired solitary chimney way down the slope on my right sent out a limp message. i didn't get it. i trudged on. the car came on. we moved to a dread encounter.

pain darts pricked my brains blood splashed the screams merged with the heat. the boy bellowed the girl cooed the man grinned and kicked me in the teeth. an orchestra. perfected choreography. the sun burned inside my skull. burned my pain dull. i suddenly fell silent. the boy cursed. he'd been about to hit the sky in climax. the girl spat a condom out of her mouth. the condom frothed at the mouth and ran away screaming for a roar of toilet water. but there was no toilet in that barrenness. it shrivelled in the heat of god's second coming, mary lay on the ground, writhing, as god came and came in an eternal orgasm. when she used her golden hair to mop up after him joseph turned his back on them. singing her virginity. and brought his rod over to me. steam rose from its head. the smell of carrion hung over it. i scream then and his rod jumped up in excitement. mary came then. the sounds of that passion smashed god 's face. for a moment his light shattered and went spasming out before my eyes. joseph's rod trod a path straight through my alimentary canal and gouged out god's light.

i crawled to the sack. they laughed at me, spurring me on. they were laughing as i snaked my way into the sackmouth. they were laughing and patting the back of each other's sadism. they were laughing as the weight of the machine brought the skin off my bloody teeth. they were laughing as i lifted it out of the hole and raised it to the sky of my shoulder. they were laughing and the thunder rolled and carried them away, in flood.

V

THE FELA SERMON

The Fela Sermon

(for Thomas Brückner)

(slave driver grave saliva
soja come soja go what he bring come forever)

1

multi-kulti dressed in mufti fela kuti's beast of no nation
rises to hold international station
what it eats swells up where it sits spills out in the street
army-arrangement-expensive-shit
human & cold on the pavement beyond martin luther king's highway
illusion dies in a trail of grey
pollution under the southern sky
gives the beast an almighty high

2

politics a capital dance   policy runs on finance
profit on the rise the fall of conscience
clean collar hearts dollar ride to sewer-side
information more than the next person
principal position of intercourse
read the gospel of saint karl marx
the cliché is a clinch it clenches around the glitch
life is a bitch yes disease & pestilence
commerce dictates you fuck her in silence

3

colonisation in revolution's disguise sows arms

both sides of conflict reaps deadly harvests
progress replaces the monstrous with its grandmother much worse
it's a truth-taking myth making death of innocence's
kiss & caress of class' cutlass
necks & axes in commerce's congress

   4

track of no foundation   bellyful of radiation
no enemy no friend   we follow the global trend
blade cutting mendicant hand
socialism's said to fail   we attach to capital's tail
smell of hell when that tail is raised
a taste of nuclear waste
radioactivity does not sate a health-thirst
it pumps full of eternal rest   in the mouth
the perennial tale of the south

   5

mattera called it a weapon   no error thereupon
stock up on the memory   terror-hawk's got an armoury
bloodstring puppetry   skins&bones sing in harmony:
what did we fight for   strike up the light for
bring the night for   wreckers of the world ignite for
who / why loot&shoot for dig down to root of scream for
         reap the do / die fruit for?
"I have a dream" of war
red like dread days of yore
yours   same as before

(slave driver grave saliva
soja come soja go what he bring come forever& evermore   AMEN)

Wailers of the world

blood-thick-beat come up mud-weak-heart bum drop everytime
run the rhyme flood sneak past bad card slick fart shark harm crop
(BEASTS & PREACHERS priests & other creatures
beavis & butthead freaks fakes two take kisses handshakes
hisses of mindsnakes i flower out of stone power from a bone)
two sevens clashed got heaven's womb slashed / torn
& I was born
another seven flashed nakasa gone
flown down a new york mental block
dove to the hawk   much love to the cock
crow on jongwe dawn
still ask why dread
i'm devil locked
each one a horn for hondo blown
tosh reception unblocked   thus read

slime stage   time page imprint
not sage i'm the message
give passage   to the lint & rage
rip off fear blinds   get lip off bare behinds
that flip & flap black-to-back-of minds' sleep of the years
now the lion's awake
hear the empire's gout run about
the valley of fears shake
like charley's princely elephant ears
peace-pipe in the snout conscience in arrears
ease wipe off terror-shout with blood & tears
seize true marley fruit (ripe) for bite of new burning spears

charisma styled on television
career-carries the child to malnutrition

number one with the wallet
hand in the air rumoured automatic
waving brain-tumour-wild arthritic / rheumatic
david sling-hot-snot king hypocrite
taught me shit
(now) wants me caught eating it
(but) scarred up barred out   tarred by rout
i remain ungovernable stain
NO poems on the production line
bone-treasure from a death-mine
the bleeding does not stop at the slaughter-stone
nor the bunny wailing hop on insane laughter's throne

dark seed   between instruction & admonition i bleed
blackness confuses sometimes
my umbilicus is surrounded by pinkness

The word or the head

        they're grabbing the gabbing
        they're nabbing the verbing

ever tramping / lamping for sanctuary
my ambition never squatter camping in the mortuary
rubber stamping my obituary
in transit at the morgue
rather prance & shit on a spiritual bog
lob the word over the head of state
& lackeys of smell & rank
than a bank job or robbery

        but they're grabbing the gabbing
        they're nabbing the verbing

should i cast my light from a great height
illuminate give sight to the locked in a state of hate
but out of sight
or crack up back-track & clock a check-mate

the choice is live in space or live with my face
& into the flow i go toe to toe with my fate

The second coming

influence become creation inspiration
in prostration
gurus will be disciples
one time principals in quickslime become pupils
i conceive mother birth father nurture earth & universe
run the order of things in reverse
like it was before it started to mean
veteran before a man
the sweep is clean
from the ripe to rotten to green
i carry broom & chalk in the classroom a rod
no award & still god to laureate & aspirant
all an apprentice in prayer mantis pose
before the rampster-presence
build shrines to my wordlines in the mind
hide before pride
same arms pushed me aside
now cramped open wide
does the noose-embrace await my head to slide inside
(bend to a friend from behind what fence?)

i burst out rest doubt the second coming
a second away from embalming mummying
nemesis in armaggedon – battle from genesis to revelations
i settle this manifestation – a golden time resurrection
the blood of this lamb gives salvation to jackals
icons turned fused beacons
the spirit gone out the fight's broken the light
silence's darknesses advance
we were loud once & then allowed to dance
& bring the noise

but the song died motions broke their poise
movers became shakers time-takers
& we knew the promisingers lied
when they turned slime-rakers
with us beneath on the ride they astride
infanticidal midwives dealing out death
choking the nation in its after-rebirth
now i bring the storm to perform
it's a clone-farm
minds wear the form
dream-state descend into the pit
wake up to find the content a uniform
drink my spit tramp in my quotable it might fit
but the stamp of light is here unduplicable
strike a match & torch now time's inflammable
i come no herald black damnation explosion
get off the scene like   aufwiedersehen

The rampster comes straight

(to the yapmaster)

(no government under any firmament worth fundament
i'm poet not ornament in cabinet / house of parliament)

anoint each line with einstein's brain
sharpen the rhyme on samson's spine
hone the rhythm on sisyphus' pain
the needle point searches for vein

assault the pen let the rage come in battery
vocabulary pierce thru vessel & artery
main in the lyrical domain
word is creation update the tradition
or fate is hysteria
with marrow of old time sun&moon warrior
make the poem arrow explode on impact
sift hype from facts
do for real what stallone acts
shift from type that'll bend to pacts
stand alone hit without special effects

lives were lost to get the vocal
fast knives come wet stay focal
critics get in rapture
but lime-light becomes crime-site
& the ones you birth wish you off the picture
how true is fickle
miss the cue show yourself true
they hiss & piss puke poison spittle
wish another one new thinks their work is too

it's another struggle stage
bungle next age same page
they spike-indict me never hike but de-mic me
even dyke me with fluffy buppie rabid puppy
chuckie acting chummy but white shark in dark facebiting
& reciting my charms
chewing & spewing to mummy to get a dummy
going yum-yummy gums tight around her harpy bummy

(no government under any firmament worth fundament
i'm poet not ornament in cabinet / house of parliament
get it   sillybitcharsellout ?)

Save the next dance

the dj says   fire for the naya
haul in pull down cool up   watch the i-a get higher

& the disc plays the sound slays the crowd sways
the lyric rocks the music cocks shocks to jam clocks

it's warm & loud on top where the dub stays
dry & heavy at the bottom the vibe flays
the mind strays down the survival maze
how long will the fun last
before the dong starts to itch
a bitch in heat come in a gun-blast
& first to burst wears the superman vest
robin hood in mean mood runs the manhood-test
blood & tears in the dirt
& the boy knows he's hurt
soon driven in a hearse
the devil's curse couldn't be worse

(they say make it walks before talks
or it's shocks out of socks
when the boat rocks goes down
my word is rocks in lead-coat on your head
make you drown
or life-line if your soul be mine)

a gun hops a child drops the music stops
fast forward to faust & save the next dance

VI

A GADIMAN LOVE SONG

A Gadiman love song

(for Shani)

I

shani shan my blue sunshine
the hungered beast leads with the horn
& out of the gored belly we were born

   python-grips on passion trips
   hips & vinelimbs entwine
   lips of wine ... skinseas & flesh-ships

sound of a hiss
the rise of the death-blow kiss
from down below jellied knees

(my pole's gone metallic to the magnetic pull
of the great hole)

moth circling around the flame of your aureole
i'm a suckling giant in this baby-role
you swallow me whole where I belly-crawl a mole
digging in the deep slipping in to sleep
in the touch & torch of your soul

II

the walls were trembling crumbling inside my being
exploding to vulvaed reeling fragments
creaming me down to filaments
raw to the root of the elements

pulling apart the nut's hairy fundament
exposing the love-nerve to lavaed feeling
electric sensation holding the air
shocking my hair from dread-lock to arrow
sucking the marrow
from my birth-bone
leaving me giving a death-groan
mid the sigh of a high tightening my fever's embrace
sticking the experience to remembrance
GIRL run come climb holy mount zion …
deft upon the flesh-rocks
crowing the sleep from unconscious cocks

III

love you in the diseased morning the moon's point of penetration
of the universe's bung-hole

love you when the sun is mortal
the days die call up cosmic death

love you in screaming scars
the sun moon & star cycle
in earth inching towards the cosmos' burning fuse
of orgasmic detonation

Printed in the United States
By Bookmasters